D1456168

Great Careers

Armed Forces

with a High School Diploma

Titles in the **Great Careers** *series*

Great Careers

Armed Forces

with a High School Diploma

Jon Sterngass

Ferguson Publishing
An imprint of Infobase Publishing

Great Careers with a High School Diploma
Armed Forces

Ferguson
An imprint of Infobase Publishing
132 West 31st Street
New York, NY 10001

ISBN-13:978-0-8160-7042-8

Library of Congress Cataloging-in-Publication Data

Great careers with a high school diploma. — 1st ed.
    v. cm.
  Includes bibliographical references and index
  Contents: [1] Food, agriculture, and natural resources — [2] Construction and trades — [3] Communications, the arts, and computers —
[4] Sales, marketing, business, and finance — [5] Personal care services, fitness, and education — [6] Health care, medicine, and science —
[7] Hospitality, human services, and tourism — [8] Public safety, law, and security — [9] Manufacturing and transportation — [10] Armed forces.
    ISBN-13: 978-0-8160-7046-6 (v.1)
    ISBN-10: 0-8160-7046-6 (v.1)
    ISBN-13: 978-0-8160-7043-5 (v.2)
    ISBN-10: 0-8160-7043-1 (v.2)
[etc.]
1. Vocational guidance — United States. 2. Occupations — United States.
3. High school graduates — Employment — United States.
  HF5382.5.U5G677 2007
  331.702'330973 — dc22
                                                          2007029883

Produced by Print Matters, Inc.
Text design by A Good Thing, Inc.
Cover design by Salvatore Luongo

Printed in the United States of America

Sheridan PMI 10 9 8 7 6 5 4 3 2 1

This book is printed on acid-free paper.

Contents

How to Use This Book

This book, part of the Great Careers with a High School Diploma series, highlights in-demand careers that require no more than a high school diploma or the general educational development (GED) credential and offer opportunities for personal growth and professional advancement to motivated readers who are looking for a field that's right for them. The focus throughout is on the fastest-growing jobs with the best potential for advancement in the field. Readers learn about future prospects while discovering jobs they may never have heard of.

Knowledge—of yourself and about a potential career—is a powerful tool in launching yourself professionally. This book tells you how to use it to your advantage, explore job opportunities, and identify a good fit for yourself in the working world.

Each chapter provides the essential information needed to find not just a job but a career that draws on your particular skills and interests. All chapters include the following features:

- ✴ "Is This Job for You?" presents a set of questions for you to answer about yourself to help you learn if you have what it takes to work in a given career.
- ✴ "Let's Talk Money" and "Lets Talk Trends" provide at a glance crucial information about salary ranges and employment prospects.
- ✴ "What You'll Do" provides descriptions of the essentials of each job.
- ✴ "Where You'll Work" relates the details of the settings and the rules and patterns typical of that field.
- ✴ "Your Typical Day" provides details about what a day on the job involves for each occupation.
- ✴ "The Inside Scoop" presents firsthand information from someone working in the field.
- ✴ "What You Can Do Now" provides advice on getting prepared for your future career.
- ✴ "What Training You'll Need" discusses state requirements, certifications, and courses or other training you may need as you get started on your new career path.
- ✴ "How to Talk Like a Pro" defines a few key terms that give a feel for the occupation.

✴ "How to Find a Job" gives the practical how-tos of landing a position.

✴ "Secrets for Success" and "Reality Check" share inside information on getting ahead.

✴ "Some Other Jobs to Think About" lists similar related careers to consider.

✴ "How You Can Move Up" outlines how people in each occupation turn a job into a career, advancing in responsibility and earnings power.

✴ "Web Sites to Surf" lists Web addresses of trade organizations and other resources providing more information about the career.

In addition to a handy comprehensive index, the back of the book features an appendix providing invaluable information on job hunting strategies and techniques. This section provides general tips on interviewing, constructing a strong résumé, and gathering professional references. Use this book to discover a career that seems right for you—the tools to get you where you want to be are at your fingertips.

Introduction

This book, highlighting 11 possible careers with the U.S. armed forces, differs from the other volumes in the Great Careers with a High School Diploma series. Quite simply, enlisting in the military is not the same as working in the civilian world, even if the job descriptions match. That's because joining the military is an enormous commitment.

Most first-term enlistments require a commitment to four years of active duty and two years of inactive duty. It is very hard to get out of the military if you change your mind after you join. You cannot simply quit, and the U.S. armed forces considers it a crime for you to leave your unit or disobey an order. A recruiter might tell you that you can try out the military and get out after just six months if you do not care for it. This is not really true. There is no such thing as an honorable discharge for "failure to adjust" in the military. What's more, planners at the Pentagon can decide to extend your tour of duty, so you may not get out when you think you will. You need to weigh any potential benefits of joining the armed forces against the fact that once you sign up, you are not entirely in control of your own life anymore. If you can deal with this and you're still interested, read on.

The U.S. armed forces is divided into five branches: the army, Marine Corps, navy, air force, and coast guard. All branches except the coast guard are part of the Department of Defense. The coast guard, the smallest of the branches, has been in several different departments. In 2003, it was moved to the Department of Homeland Security, but it operates under the Department of Defense in time of war.

As of 2007, there were more than 1.4 million people serving in the U.S. military. An additional 1.2 million are in the reserves.

The U.S. armed forces is a voluntary military. That means that there is no conscription (draft), and no one is forced to serve. Because of this, the military constantly has to recruit the people to fill its more than one million positions. You've seen the advertisements. They promise job training, money for college, adventure, and leadership skills. It is crucial to remember, however, that military recruiters are basically salespeople. Their job is to convince you to enlist. Most recruiters have to sign up a certain quota of people each month in order to advance their careers. During periods when joining the military is not a popular option, such as when the United States is fighting a

Total Active Duty Personnel (as of May 2007)

Service	Total personnel	Percent of total armed services personnel	Percentage of each service that is female
Army	507,000	36%	14%
Marine Corps	180,000	13%	6%
Navy	341,000	24%	15%
Air Force	341,000	24%	20%
Coast Guard	41,000	3%	11%

war, the pressure on recruiters intensifies. In those times, recruiters stress the benefits of military service and place less emphasis on the drawbacks.

On the one hand, there are real benefits to joining the military. They include:

✯ **Job training** The military offers thousands of specialized jobs in a wide variety of fields. You don't have to be in the infantry. Almost 90 percent of military jobs have direct civilian counterparts, and most of these are noncombat occupations. Of course, the numbers don't tell the whole story. That's because, according to the military, all positions are potentially combat positions. However, the current ratio of combat to noncombat troops is usually about 1:2 or 1:3.

✯ **Educational benefits** The U.S. armed forces offer excellent educational benefits. After your tour of enlistment is over, you can collect more than $25,000 from the Montgomery GI Bill for your education. There are also several other educational support programs, which, if added together, can total more than $70,000 in tuition benefits.

✯ **Fringe benefits** As a member of the military, you get free medical and dental care, free gym and exercise facilities, free on-base housing (if available), and 30 days of vacation with pay.

✯ **Travel** Moving on is a way of life in the military. You might be sent somewhere in the United States or perhaps anywhere around the world. A popular U.S. Navy recruiting slogan remains, "Join the navy—see the world."

✴ **Career** In the military, you earn a steady paycheck from the moment you sign up. If you join at age 18, you can serve a full 20 years and retire at age 38!

✴ **Sense of purpose** As a member of the U.S. armed forces, you are part of an organization that is important in the world. You're not working just to make money and acquire more consumer junk. Ideally, you're helping to defend the national security of the United States.

On the other hand, there are definite disadvantages to joining the U.S. armed forces. The first drawback is obvious; you may be killed or seriously injured. Similarly, you may have to kill someone else whom you don't know and with whom you don't have a personal quarrel. In some eras, this was a remote possibility. In others, such as during the Vietnam War or the Gulf Wars in Iraq, the chances increased dramatically. The main purpose of the military is to fight; if you want the benefits, you may have to walk the walk.

In addition, the military is not for every type of personality, especially if you have trouble following orders. The U.S. armed forces is rigidly hierarchical, and respect for the authority of all higher-ranking people is a core principle. As a member, you have to assume and trust that higher-ranking people are acting in your (and the nation's) best interest. If the United States goes to war, you have to fight regardless of your personal views. Once you enlist, you can't choose whether to take up arms.

Before you decide to enlist, look carefully at what you will actually be doing. Jobs with fancy sounding titles often hide low-skill and nontechnical positions. Some military jobs are so different from their civilian counterparts that you may have to be retrained after you leave the military. Most important, the military is not required to keep you full time in the job for which you trained. Nor do they have to keep you in it for the entire time you are in the military. Keep in mind as well that some advanced training programs require additional service commitments or additional active duty time.

If you do not like to travel, the armed forces is probably not for you. Military units in all services can be deployed away from homeports, bases, or airfields at any time. As of 2005, the United States occupied more than 700 military bases in more than 35 countries around the world. Some of the largest contingents were in Iraq, Germany, Japan, South Korea, Afghanistan, Italy, and the United Kingdom.

It's true that joining the military is a way to "serve your country." However, it is not the only way, and it is not unpatriotic to pass on military service. Fighting fires or helping students in an inner city aids the country as much as driving a forklift on an airbase in Germany. The ultimate value of military service is a judgment only each individual can make for him- or herself. This does not mean you shouldn't enlist. Simply do not enlist unless you are sure this is the right choice for you. Your decision will affect your own life, the lives of your family members, and possibly, the lives of many other people.

If you do decide to enlist, don't sign any papers until you take them home for a parent, teacher, or someone else you trust to review them. When you enlist, you sign an enlistment contract. This contract determines your initial commitment, signing bonuses, job-training guarantees, and any other incentives. Make absolutely sure to get all the recruiter's promises in writing in your enlistment agreement. No oral agreement you made with the recruiter is binding; it has to be in writing. Find out whether you need to pass a special test, get a security clearance, or do anything else before you can get the job or options you want.

Remember, there are slightly different enlistment requirements for each branch. However, minimum entrance age requirements for the U.S. armed forces are a standard 17 years of age with parental consent or 18 years of age without parental consent.

Physical requirements for each branch of the service also vary and can differ even within a branch for various subcategories of troops. In general, enlistees should be in good physical condition, of appropriate weight, and able to pass a standard physical screening prior to entry. If you report to basic training too out of shape to train with the others, you may be placed in a separate remedial physical fitness program. Spare yourself the embarrassment and make sure you're in decent shape beforehand.

You have a better chance of getting your military job of choice if you have a high school diploma. Candidates with a credential of general educational development (GED) can enlist, but some services may limit their opportunities. Without a high school diploma or equivalent, you're more than likely bound for the infantry or a similarly unskilled position.

After you enlist, you will be sent for some form of "basic training," as the U.S. Army calls it. Terminology for all training tends to vary from branch to branch. Of course, enlistees have their own choice words for it. Basic training is a rough program of physical

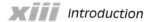

To join the . . .	You must:
Air Force	Be between the ages of 17 and 27. Have no more than two dependents. Take the Armed Services Vocational Aptitude Battery test (ASVAB). (Minimum AFQT Score: 36)
Army	Be between the ages of 17 and 42. Have no more than two dependents. Take the Armed Services Vocational Aptitude Battery test. (Minimum AFQT Score: 31)
Coast Guard	Be between the ages of 17 and 27. Have no more than two dependents. Take the Armed Services Vocational Aptitude Battery test. (Minimum AFQT Score: 36) Have a willingness to serve on or around the water.
Marines	Be between the ages of 17 and 29. Take the Armed Services Vocational Aptitude Battery test. (Minimum AFQT Score: 32) Meet physical and moral standards.
Navy	Be between the ages of 17 and 34. Take the Armed Services Vocational Aptitude Battery test. (Minimum AFQT Score: 35)

and mental training required to join the military. It is carried out at several different bases around the United States. Basic training can last anywhere from nine weeks to more than one year, depending on the career a person chooses on enlistment. Despite its reputation for difficulty, about 90 percent of recruits successfully complete basic training.

Advanced Individual Training (AIT), another army term, makes up the rest of the training period. In the AIT (again, the terminology varies from branch to branch), recruits train to become experts in their chosen field (sometimes known as "military occupational specialty," or "MOS"). Therefore, the length of AIT differs depending on what specialty you select. If an individual choses to enlist as a food service specialist, then some of their AIT would be spent at the U.S. Army Quartermaster Center and School at Fort Lee, Virginia. However, a person who choses law enforcement and security would probably train at Fort Leonard Wood in Missouri, home of the Military Police School. In general, each branch has its own advanced individual training programs. Although advanced training schools do not center on combat, enlistees are still subject to the same duties, strict daily schedule, and disciplinary rules as in basic training.

The range of possible military careers is quite broad and it would take an extremely long book to cover all of them. This volume highlights careers in the U.S. armed forces that are available at an entry level with only a high school diploma. Some of these jobs will be familiar, and others unfamiliar. The book attempts to cover a fairly wide range of specialties to give you a feeling for the range of possibilities of military enlistment. Don't forget that most of these jobs are available in at least four of the five branches and that they might differ somewhat from branch to branch.

Some of these military specialties, such as personnel specialist or law enforcement and security specialist, require relatively little academic study. Others, such as aircraft mechanic or medical service technician, require extensive training. Many military careers are becoming increasingly complex. However, the benefit of joining the military is that you don't need to spend four years in a classroom to learn these job skills. Instead, you can learn them on the job.

If you are reading this book, you understand that pursuing something besides a college degree after high school makes sense for many people. College is expensive, and costs continue to rise much faster than inflation. Many individuals cannot afford the thousands of dollars needed to get a degree. The U.S. military offer programs with two-, three- and six-year active duty, or reserve enlistments. It depends upon the branch and the job that you want. For the right person, it is a viable alternative to college.

There is a wide range of exciting and satisfying military careers available without a college diploma. In addition, there is no rule that says that you can't go back to college later in life, in five, ten, or even twenty years. In most cases, the military will help defray at least part of the cost. If you can deal with the commitment and the mission, then perhaps this is the route for you.

Track huge sums of money

Finance and Accounting Specialist

Keep payrolls and supply orders moving smoothly

Prevent fraud and waste

Finance and Accounting Specialist

When young people think of the U.S. military, images of tanks, battles, aerial dogfights, and urban patrols come to mind. It's easy to forget that working for the U.S. armed forces is also a job. People who work for the military, whether they are soldiers or suppliers, have to be paid. That's where finance and accounting specialists come in. Each year, the military services spend billions and issue millions of paychecks for personnel, equipment, and supplies. As with any business, someone has to keep exact financial records of all these transactions. Finance and accounting specialists record, organize, and track these records. They also audit accounts to make sure that the military handles the taxpayer's money efficiently and legally. This is a job for anyone who loves math.

Is This Job for You?

Would working as a finance and accounting specialist be a good fit for you? To find out, read each of the following statements and answer "Yes" or "No."

Yes	No	**1.**	Do you enjoy work that emphasizes accuracy?
Yes	No	**2.**	Do you pay attention to small details?
Yes	No	**3.**	Can you keep privileged information private?
Yes	No	**4.**	Do you have good communication skills?
Yes	No	**5.**	Do you enjoy using computers and calculators?
Yes	No	**6.**	Are you comfortable working at a desk all day?
Yes	No	**7.**	Are you trustworthy?
Yes	No	**8.**	Are you well organized?
Yes	No	**9.**	Do you like to work with numbers?
Yes	No	**10.**	Are you able to check your own work to find errors?

If you answered "Yes" to most of these questions, you might consider a career as a finance and accounting specialist. To find out more about this job, read on.

What You'll Do

As a finance and accounting specialist, you would control the flow of money in the U.S. armed forces by maintaining exact financial records of all transactions. You would do this by planning, organizing, tracking,

Let's Talk Money

Personnel with one to three years of service in the armed forces earn from $16,000 to $20,000 per year in base salary. Benefits—including health care, tuition support, career training, and life insurance—are excellent. Most soldiers on active duty also receive a housing allowance, a subsistence allowance, combat pay, and other benefits. If you qualify as a finance and accounting specialist, you may be eligible for up to a $40,000 enlistment bonus. In civilian life, bookkeepers make between about $20,000 and $50,000 a year, according to 2006 U.S. Bureau of Labor Statistics data.

balancing, and projecting military finances, budgets, and payments. You'd maintain accounting records, including keeping track of expenses, money received, and accounts payable and receivable.

Finance and accounting specialists are the military's financial record keepers. They also make purchases, prepare invoices, and keep track of overdue accounts. You could be buying bananas or bullets, gasoline or grapefruit. Or you might be watching over multimillion-dollar oil well reconstruction projects. You may organize information on past expenses to help plan military budgets for future expenses. One of your main jobs would be to prepare paychecks and handle the payroll. You'd disburse cash, checks, and advance pay.

The job also involves detective-type work. You could be assigned to monitor budgets and review or audit financial records to check the accuracy of figures and calculations. This ensures that funds are being properly used. You would carefully examine statements, bills, invoices, and other financial accounts and reports to make certain that all the information appearing on them is accurate and complete. Then you might prepare reports and summaries for higher officers.

Each day, you would make hundreds of computations. Many aspects of your job that used to be done by hand are now performed using computers and spreadsheets. Numbers are rarely entered into a general ledger manually anymore. You'd need to be able to work comfortably with computers to perform calculations, record details of financial transactions, and maintain accounting records. Though it's true you have to know or learn these skills, they make working with numbers so much easier than 30 years ago.

Who You'll Work For

* ⭐ Army
* ⭐ Navy
* ⭐ Air force
* ⭐ Marine Corps
* ⭐ Coast guard

Where You'll Work

Finance and accounting specialists work in offices on land or aboard ships. You may be stationed somewhere in the United States or anywhere around the world. You might even be sent to a battle zone.

Even if you were stationed in a combat zone, you wouldn't be likely to get fired on at your desk. Finance and accounting specialists sit for extended periods while reviewing detailed data. This can lead to eye and muscle strain, backaches, headaches, and repetitive motion injuries.

Finance and accounting specialists, like their peers in the civilian work force, usually work 9 a.m. to 5 p.m. and a standard 40-hour week. However, they may work longer hours to meet deadlines or during large-scale military operations. Civilian bookkeepers and accounting clerks may work overtime at the end of the fiscal year, during tax time, or when performing large accounting audits. Those who work in hotels, restaurants, and stores may put in long hours during peak holiday and vacation seasons.

Let's Talk Trends

Both the military and civilian work forces always need bookkeepers. In 2004, bookkeepers and accounting clerks held more than two million civilian and military jobs. They work in every industry and type of business. Although computers now perform many financial and accounting functions, the enormous size of this occupation ensures plentiful job openings. However, according to the Bureau of Labor Statistics, the employment of bookkeeping and accounting clerks is projected to grow more slowly than average for all occupations through 2014.

The Inside Scoop: Q&A

Travelle Wright
Chief of financial management
Buckley Air Force Base, Aurora, Colorado

Q: *How did you get your job?*

A: I [met] a former Tuskegee airman. The more he talked about his experiences, the more interested I became in the air force. He suggested that I try out the Air Force Reserve Officer's Training Corps (ROTC). I signed up for a class and I loved it.

Q: *What do you like best about your job?*

A: Currently, I am the chief of financial management at the Aerospace Data Facility (ADF). The ADF is a space tracking and data processing center that monitors information from satellites across the globe . . . I take care of the day-to-day finances of the ADF . . . I take part in monthly meetings about the budget . . . I need to analyze each situation individually and then decide if the budget needs to be revised for a particular program.

Q: *What is the most challenging parts of your job?*

A: [At] Peterson Air Force Base in Colorado . . . I was responsible for the travel office, the military pay office, and the account and liaison office. This was an interesting and very challenging job because I dealt directly with personnel and their financial matters. I had to make tough decisions about travel expense reimbursement, for example, and relay these decisions to personnel.

Q: *What are the keys to success to being an accounting specialist?*

A: Throughout my career, I've found that the military demands a high level of responsibility from its personnel. The responsibility that I've been entrusted with over my 15-year career has enabled me to explore my career field fully and given me great opportunities to learn leadership skills.

Your Typical Day

Here are some highlights for a typical day as a finance and accounting specialist.

✓ **Prepare the payroll.** A typical aircraft carrier handles a payroll of more than $2 million every two weeks. As a sailor in the finance and accounting field, you devote a substantial part of your time each week to ensuring that the everyone is paid the correct amount and on time.

✓ **Provide and account for supplies.** All branches need a constant stream of supplies and spare parts to keep running. Today you are ordering additional munitions and protective gear.

✓ **Audit records.** Every tax dollar spent is supposed to be accounted for in the U.S. armed forces. You'll have to accurately track every penny by carefully checking other peoples' work. This afternoon, you're investigating several bills that may have been overpaid.

What You Can Do Now

★ Take math classes in high school. Don't even consider this field if you don't like math. Other useful subjects include bookkeeping, accounting, and business classes.

★ Brush up on your computer skills. Make sure you know how to use computers and calculators. Knowledge of word processing and spreadsheet software will also give you an edge. You can always take a class at a community college to learn or review these skills.

★ Work or intern in an office environment. Experience counts for a lot when it comes to getting your career choice in the military. A finance- or accounting-related job or even a nonpaying internship will help you be selected for this position in the military.

What Training You'll Need

Basic training for most of the branches of the armed forces is about 10 weeks. Depending on the branch, you might be required to learn the proper use of firearms as well as uniform standards and military knowledge and courtesy. After you successfully complete basic training, you would progress to advanced initial training where you will be trained to be a finance and accounting specialist.

Most of your job training for the position of finance and accounting specialist will take place in a classroom. This might take about eight weeks but training length depends on your specialty. You'll have to review or relearn the information usually covered in accounting and math classes in high school. You'll cover accounting principles and procedures, the preparation of financial reports and budgets, interpreting financial data using statistical analyses, and the proper way to figure out pay and deductions.

As the military continues to computerize financial records, you'll learn to use specialized accounting computer software on personal computers. Records such as receipts or bills are now entered on computer spreadsheets and databases. The information is then stored either electronically or as computer printouts (or both). A major part of your training will be mastering specific computer software programs.

After your classroom training is completed, you will usually receive on-the-job training, during which you'll learn the typical procedures of your unit from an experienced officer or senior worker. She or he will help you with the practical knowledge needed to do your job efficiently and accurately.

How to Talk Like a Pro

Here are a few words you'll hear in this career:

- ✴ **Accounts payable (A/P)** The record of what your unit owes for goods or services.
- ✴ **Audit** An audit is a critical examination of accounting procedures and financial statements. Its purpose is to decide if financial statements are accurate. An audit can also establish whether transactions have been recorded properly.
- ✴ **Bookkeeping** Bookkeeping is the basic method of recording business dealings. This involves keeping track of dates, sums, money coming in, and expenses.

How to Find a Job

Many young men and women enlist in the armed forces right out of high school. An 18-year old high school graduate can walk into the local recruiter's office and enlist. Seventeen-year-olds can also enlist but need a parent's permission.

To serve in the U.S. military, a person must pass physical requirements and a background check. Academically, an applicant must score at least a 31 on the Armed Forces Qualification Test (AFQT), a test given to everyone who enlists. For the army, your service obligations would be determined at the recruiter's office. You can agree with the recruiter to serve for two, three, four, or even five years. Be aware that you may be guaranteed training in your field of choice, but not a job in it.

Secrets for Success

See the following suggestions and turn to the appendix for advice on résumés and interviews.

- ✴ It's all in the details. Finance and accounting work requires an almost obsessive concern with details and with making numbers add up. If you have this skill and desire, you're more than halfway there.
- ✴ No matter the discipline, every job is social. Keep a golden rule of being aware of those around you.

Reality Check

As a finance and accounting specialist you're on a career path to sit at a desk and crunch numbers for most of your life. It's not a profession for everyone.

Some Other Jobs to Think About

- ✴ Defense Finance and Accounting Service (DFAS) accountant. Working for the DFAS is the civilian equivalent of being a finance and accounting specialist. The DFAS, the world's largest finance and accounting organization, has about 15,000 civilian employees who provide financial and accounting services for the Department of Defense military services.
- ✴ Procurement clerks. Procurement clerks put together requests for materials. They also prepare purchase orders, keep track of purchases and supplies, and handle questions about orders.
- ✴ Tellers. Tellers usually work in banks. The job has a similar emphasis on attention to detail, honesty, and trustworthiness. For this position, however, you have to deal with the public.

How You Can Move Up

⭐ Advance in the military. In the armed forces, promotions can come quickly based on time in service and merit. After four years, you can become a senior finance and accounting officer. Among other duties, these officers plan, develop, and coordinate budgets for their unit. After 15 years, you can advance to finance and accounting director. These officers monitor large budgets, disburse money, and oversee internal controls to ensure the proper use of funds.

⭐ Advance in civilian life. In civilian life, finance and accounting specialists are known as accounting clerks, audit clerks, bookkeepers, or payroll clerks. With experience and education, it is possible to become an accountant or auditor, although jobs in these specialties usually require a college degree.

Web Sites to Surf

Careers in the Military. This Web site is the starting point for any investigation of jobs in the armed forces. It includes many useful job descriptions and links. http://www.careersinthemilitary.com

Today's Military. This site gives in-depth information on each branch of the U.S. armed forces. http://www.todaysmilitary.com

American Institute of Professional Bookkeepers. The institute, founded in 1987, is the bookkeeping profession's national association. Its Web site has many useful links about the profession. http://www.aipb.org

Construct dams and buildings

Construction Equipment Operator

Drive and control bulldozers, graders, and other heavy equipment

Build and maintain roads and airfields

Construction Equipment Operator

When you were young, did you get a kick from playing with toy dump trucks and tractors? Does the idea of operating heavy equipment still fascinate you? Each year, the U.S. armed forces completes hundreds of building and maintenance projects around the world. Military workers move tons of earth to construct airfields, roads, dams, and buildings. They deliver building materials to a site and then place them in the proper position. These are all tasks that require construction equipment operators. These specialists drive bulldozers, graders, and other heavy equipment to cut and level earth for runways and roadbeds. They also operate smaller equipment such as air compressors and pneumatic tools. The job is a dream come true for people who loved to play with toy vehicles and machines as kids.

Is This Job for You?

Would working as a construction equipment operator be a good fit for you? To find out, read each of the following questions and answer "Yes" or "No."

Yes	*No*	**1.**	Do you like to work outdoors?
Yes	*No*	**2.**	Do you enjoy a job that allows you to use your hands?
Yes	*No*	**3.**	Are you interested in operating construction equipment?
Yes	*No*	**4.**	Do you like to build things?
Yes	*No*	**5.**	Do you have a good sense of balance?
Yes	*No*	**6.**	Are you detail-oriented?
Yes	*No*	**7.**	Do you like tinkering with machines?
Yes	*No*	**8.**	Can you work under conditions that may be noisy and uncomfortable?
Yes	*No*	**9.**	Are you in good physical condition?
Yes	*No*	**10.**	Do you have good hand-eye-foot coordination?

If you answered "Yes" to most of these questions, you might consider a career as a construction equipment operator. To find out more about this job, read on.

Let's Talk Money

Compensation in the military is primarily based on years of service. A private with one year in the armed forces draws an income of about $16,000 annually, whereas a corporal with three years' service earns about $20,000 per year. Government benefits are famously excellent and include career training, health care, some money for college, and life insurance. Most soldiers on active duty also receive further compensation. In civilian life, construction equipment operators have a mean annual salary of $39,290, according to 2006 data from the U.S. Bureau of Labor Statistics.

What You'll Do

As a military construction equipment operator, you will repair or build structures. You will use any of many different machines, both large and small, to construct airfields, dams, bridges, roads, and buildings. You might operate trucks, bulldozers, backhoes, forklifts, piledrivers, graders, or cranes to clear and grade land and prepare it for construction.

You might operate a tractor crawler—which has tracks instead of wheels, to suit it for use on soft ground, mud, and snow. Using a tractor crawler, you might construct embankments and excavate hills and slopes, or you might use it for cleaning, stripping, backfilling, stockpiling, or pushing a scraper.

Other commonly used machines include control power shovels, which are used to dig holes and trenches to lay or repair sewer and other pipelines. Excavation and loading machines equipped with scoops, shovels, or buckets are operated to dig sand, gravel, and earth and load it into trucks. You could use winches, cranes, and hoists to lift and move heavy construction materials.

General construction equipment operators use air compressors, pumps, and pneumatic tools. They also operate specialized construction machines that pump, compact, ditch, and augur. And don't forget that the heavy construction equipment itself needs to be transported to and from a site using a tractor-trailer.

Another area of construction is paving roads or airfields using asphalt or concrete. Tamping equipment operators run machines that compact earth and other materials for roadbeds. Concrete-paving machine operators control machines that spread, vibrate, and level wet concrete in forms. They use other attachments to smooth the surface of the concrete, spray on a curing compound, and cut expansion joints. Construction equipment operation is a huge field with many choices, both in and out of the military.

Who You'll Work For

✯ All five service branches. The army, navy, air force, Marine Corps, and coast guard all use construction equipment operators.

✯ Construction and maintenance units. Military construction equipment operators often work in specific units.

✯ The Seabees. The Seabees, founded during World War II, are the construction units of the U.S. Navy. They have built hundreds of bases and bulldozed and paved thousands of miles of roadway and airstrips. Their unofficial motto is "Can Do!"

Where You'll Work

Most military construction equipment operators work outdoors. They often get muddy, dusty, or greasy while working in nearly every type of climate and weather condition. Military operations cannot stop just because it is scorching hot, freezing cold, or sopping wet. For example, you might have to remove ice and snow from runways, roads, and other northern or mountainous areas using scrapers and snow blowers. This means operators will be chilled in the winter and overheated in the summer. However, operators might occasionally work indoors while repairing equipment.

Some operators work in remote locations—such as Iceland, Guam, or Turkey—on large construction projects like highways and

Let's Talk Trends

In civilian life, construction is one of the nation's largest industries. It employs more than 7 million people; about 450,000 of them operate construction equipment. The job market in civilian construction obviously depends on the economy. However, employment is expected to increase with population and business growth. Prospects for military workers will be steady as long as there is money for the services.

dams, or in factory or mining operations. The U.S. armed forces is involved all around the world, and you might be sent anywhere. Be prepared to move.

Operators may work irregular hours because work on some construction projects continues around the clock. Construction work might have to be performed late at night or early in the morning. This is especially true if you are involved in working in a combat zone. In general, however, construction equipment operation works a standard schedule.

Your Typical Day

Here are some highlights for a typical day as a construction equipment operator working with asphalt.

✔ **Consult with the mixing plant to make asphalt.** Mixing the asphalt correctly is very important. Without the asphalt mixed in the proper proportions, a crew could not build a quality roadway. You assist the hot-plant operator to make sure the proper mix is produced.

✔ **Transport the asphalt to the site.** You are in charge of transferring the 300-degree-Fahrenheit asphalt from the silo to the site. You wear personal protective equipment and watch out for burns, spills, falls, explosions, and over-fills.

✔ **Spread the asphalt.** To build the road, the asphalt has to be dumped, spread, and leveled. You operate the paving machine to control the temperature and flow of asphalt onto the roadbed. You make sure that the asphalt-paving machine distributes the paving material evenly and doesn't leave empty spaces.

What You Can Do Now

✯ Take relevant classes in high school. Helpful subjects include automobile and shop mechanics, science, and mechanical drawing.

✯ Take a class at a vocational school. Vocational schools often teach the operation of some types of construction equipment. Completion of such programs, or even a class, gives an applicant a definite advantage when it comes to getting the specialty requested.

✯ Get some real experience. Experience operating related equipment, such as farm tractors or heavy equipment, is a huge asset.

The Inside Scoop: Q&A

Robert Sheipline
Structural specialist, vertical repair shop
Bolling Air Force Base, Washington, D.C.

Q: *How did you get your job?*

A: My dad was in the air force for four years and talked about it a lot. I decided to give the air force a chance. I planned on being in the service for four years, but now I've been in for 12 years and have established a career. I'm also close to finishing my associate's degree in construction technology.

When I came into the air force, I was young, active, and athletic. I wanted to work outside and work with my hands. By the time that I finished basic training, they had combined some career fields, so at tech school I also learned carpentry, masonry, welding, and sheet metal work. My first assignment [included] a lot of facility maintenance but I was eager to do more major construction work. A senior airman suggested that I volunteer for an overseas assignment to gain more experience. I ended up going to Okinawa [Japan] for six years.

Q: *What do you like best about your job?*

A: My best experience was in Honduras where we were part of a humanitarian mission and built a maternity clinic in the poor town of Jutiapa . . . I [especially like the] travel and career opportunities.

Q: *What's the most challenging part of your job?*

A I was in Iraq in 2003 and did site survey work for the National Intelligence Center (NIC). It was the early stage of the Iraq war, and they needed everything from communication lines to basic power. We were living out of one of the palaces and I rigged up an air conditioning unit, using formica and duct tape to make duct work.

(Continued on next page)

(continued from previous page)

Q: *What are the keys to success to being a construction equipment operator?*

A: In addition to the construction and managerial skills that I've developed in the air force, I've also learned the importance of teamwork. In many situations, your life is on the line, so teamwork is essential.

What Training You'll Need

Job training for a military construction equipment operator begins with about nine weeks of basic training. In basic training, recruits learn basic soldiering skills. This is followed by four to 12 weeks of advanced individual training, depending on the job classification. You'll spend part of this time in the classroom and part in the field.

In the classroom, you'll learn about the operation of different types of construction equipment and vehicles. You might specialize in one type of machine in the armed forces, but you also might have to know how to operate several different types. You will also learn how to set up and inspect the equipment, make mechanical adjustments, and perform some maintenance and minor repairs.

However, construction equipment operators usually learn most of their skills on the job. You'll probably start by operating light equipment while an experienced operator looks on. Later you may operate heavier equipment such as bulldozers and cranes.

The operation of construction equipment is becoming more complicated. Technologically advanced construction equipment uses computerized controls and complex hydraulics and electronics. Global Positioning System (GPS) technology now helps with grading and leveling activities. These newer machines require more skill to operate. If you plan to operate this type of equipment, you may need additional training and some understanding of electronics.

You can apply most of the training you receive in the military to credit hours towards a college degree. You might also have the opportunity for continued education through various college programs or tuition assistance. There are several three-year apprenticeship programs for which you may qualify. These programs, run by the International Union of Operating Engineers and the Associated General Contractors of America, consist of at least three years or 6,000 hours of on-the-job training and 144 hours per year of classroom instruction.

All of these skills are easily transmitted to the civilian job market if you want to do so. Whether in the military or the civilian world, construction equipment operators use their combined efficiency, teamwork, and reliability to build almost anything in any place.

How to Talk Like a Pro

Here are a few words you'll hear in this career:

★ **Backfill** The replacement of excavated earth into a trench around and against a basement foundation.

★ **Backhoe** A backhoe is a self-powered excavation machine that digs by pulling a boom-mounted bucket towards itself. A backhoe digs foundations and footings and helps install drainage or sewer systems.

★ **Pile driver** A large machine, mounted on skids, barges, or cranes, that hammers piles into the ground. Piles are long, heavy beams of wood or steel driven into the ground to support retaining walls, piers, or building foundations.

How to Find a Job

Many young men and women enlist in the armed forces right out of high school. For an 18-year old graduate, the step consists of nothing more than paying a visit to the local armed forces recruiting office.

To serve in the U.S. military, a person must pass physical requirements and a background check. For the army, your service obligations would be determined at the recruiter's office. You can agree with the recruiter to serve for two, three, four, or even five years. Job specialties are subject to availability and an applicant's qualifications. As with all jobs, some previous experience in the field will move you towards the head of the list.

Secrets for Success

See the following suggestions and turn to the appendix for advice on résumés and interviews.

★ Be willing to travel. Many construction equipment operator jobs involve traveling around the world with the U.S. armed forces. Some people prefer this type of life with its frequent moves, others do not.

✴ Practice makes perfect. Volunteer with the local parks department to get experience working with machines.

Reality Check

Operating construction equipment is a little like driving a car. It is exciting at first but may grow tedious after a time. So imagine driving a bulldozer for your career. You will be sitting for long periods of time. Heavy machinery is noisy and shakes or jolts the operator. Operating it can also be dangerous.

Some Other Jobs to Think About

✴ Truck drivers; agricultural equipment operators. These civilian careers offer the opportunity to operate heavy mechanical equipment outside of the construction industry. Truck drivers are also needed by the U.S. armed forces.

✴ Carpenters, electricians, plumbers. These jobs are all construction positions that do not usually involve the operation of large mechanical equipment. They're perfect for people who like to build things.

✴ Automobile mechanic. An excellent job for problem solvers who enjoy tinkering with machines.

How You Can Move Up

✴ Advance in the military. In the armed forces, promotions can come quickly based on time in service and merit. After four years, you can become a crew leader. Among other duties, these officers oversee teams of construction specialists. They interpret drawings and blueprints to plan and lay out work. After 19 years, you can advance to "trades superintendent." Trades superintendents supervise large construction and maintenance units.

✴ Advance in civilian life. The ability to operate several different types of construction equipment makes you more valuable and is usually a step to higher pay. This may require taking some extra classes at a vocational school. Beyond this, operators move to crew leaders or contractors. The construction skills that you learn in the armed forces, in addition to leadership training, will help advance your career. About three out of five civilian equipment operators work for the construction industry. Another fifth work for state or local governments. Others work for mining, manufacturing, or utility companies. Less than 5 percent of equipment operators are self-employed.

Web Sites to Surf

Careers in the Military. This Web site is the starting point for any investigation of jobs in the armed forces. It includes many useful job descriptions and links. http://www.careersinthemilitary.com

Today's Military. This site gives in-depth information on each branch of the U.S. armed forces. http://www.todaysmilitary.com

National Center for Construction Education and Research. The center is an education foundation affiliated with the University of Florida. The Web site has useful information about training and safety programs. http://www.nccer.org/index.asp

Fix broken electrical equipment

Electrical Equipment Repairer

Troubleshoot and solve challenging problems

Use cutting-edge technology

Electrical Equipment Repairer

Electricity powers most of the equipment used by the U.S. armed forces. Whether it's a vehicle or a machine, chances are that electrical equipment repairers fix, maintain, or inspect it. Electric motors, electric tools, and medical equipment need precision maintenance and repair. The world's most advanced weaponry, ships, and aircraft could not operate without electricity. All of these systems need to be maintained by service men and women to enable the military to function. If you are fascinated by circuits, electrical work, and electronics, then electrical equipment repair might be the field for you.

Is This Job for You?

Would working as an electrical equipment repairer be a good fit for you? To find out, read each of the following questions and answer "Yes" or "No."

Yes No **1.** Do you like to work with your hands?

Yes No **2.** Do you like doing physical work?

Yes No **3.** Could you see yourself confidently working on multimillion dollar machinery?

Yes No **4.** Are you interested in how electrical equipment works?

Yes No **5.** Do you work accurately, and with attention to detail?

Yes No **6.** Are you confident enough to work with high voltage electricity?

Yes No **7.** Are you mechanically inclined?

Yes No **8.** Are you a good problem solver?

Yes No **9.** Do you enjoy studying math and shop mechanics in school?

Yes No **10.** Do you keep your cool under pressure?

If you answered "Yes" to most of these questions, you might consider a career as an electrical equipment repairer. To find out more about this job, read on.

Let's Talk Money

Military jobs pay according to seniority, with privates and corporals—with one and three years' service, respectively—earning base salaries of $16,000 and $20,000 per year, respectively. Military benefits include career training, health care, money for college, and life insurance. In civilian life, electricians have annual average earnings of more than $46,620, according to 2006 data from the U.S. Bureau of Labor Statistics.

What You'll Do

The field of electrical repair is so large that it almost defies a job description. The military uses electricity to do countless jobs, including lighting hospitals, running power tools, and operating computers. In addition, every military base, no matter where in the world, has its own electrical supply. This creates thousands of jobs for military electricians.

As an electrical equipment repairer, you would be responsible for repairing electrical systems in offices, repair shops, airplane hangars, ships, and other buildings. When breakdowns occur, you would make the necessary repairs as quickly as possible in order to reduce inconvenience and protect the integrity of the facility. You might have to replace items or install new circuit breakers, fuses, switches, or wire. Then you would test the repair to make sure the system was operational and safe.

However, because electricity is so widely used in the armed forces, there are hundreds of other possibilities with regard to your duties. You may routinely inspect, maintain, and repair some of the most technologically advanced communications, navigation, and combat-systems equipment in the world. Alternatively, you might be fixing portable electric tools such as saws and drills. Much depends on your training and area of expertise.

Some of your work might be specific to the military. You might have to repair devices such as night-vision equipment or battlefield illumination devices. You might also study the electrical systems aboard a Seahawk helicopter. Someone has to repair the nuclear, biological, and chemical warning and measuring devices. You might even be fixing the complex electrical systems for guided missiles and their launching systems.

However, a great deal of the job is the standard electrical work that transfers easily to the civilian world. You would repair electric motors, generators, switchboards, and control equipment as well as power and lighting circuits and electrical fixtures. You may also inspect and repair electrical, medical, and dental equipment, as well as instruments such as voltmeters, temperature gauges, and altimeters (an instrument that registers changes in atmospheric pressure to measure altitude). You would read blueprints, manuals, and technical diagrams to locate damaged parts of generators and control equipment and repair them. Whatever you work on, the job of an electrical equipment repairer requires excellent problem-solving skills and technical ability.

Who You'll Work For

✯ All five branches. The army, navy, air force, Marine Corps, and coast guard all need electrical equipment repairers.

✯ The Seabees. This navy construction battalion provides the crucial link between land and naval forces by constructing buildings, ports, and other structures required for ships, aircraft, machinery, and personnel.

Where You'll Work

Because of the common need for electrical services, electrical equipment repairers can be found in all parts of the military and all over the world. For example, you might work in a repair shop aboard a ship, on a military base in the United States, or at an airfield in a combat zone.

Electrical equipment repairers work both indoors and outdoors. Repair work has to happen regardless of the weather. This means you may be working in the 110-degree sun or in below-zero temperatures.

Let's Talk Trends

Anything with wiring, gears, or other parts eventually breaks down. Electricians held more than 600,000 jobs in 2007, and the Bureau of Labor Statistics projects that employment in the field should increase as fast as average through the year 2014. Nearly two-thirds of electricians worked in the construction industry.

The work can sometimes be strenuous. You might have to lift heavy objects and stand, stoop, and kneel for long periods.

Most electricians work a standard 40-hour week, although you may have to work additional hours for major projects. You may have to work nights, weekends, and holidays. You may also spend time on call, ready to drop whatever you're doing and race to the worksite.

Your Typical Day

Here are some highlights for a typical day as an electrical equipment repairer (or "electrician's mate") aboard a U.S. Coast Guard cutter.

✓ **Perform scheduled maintenance.** A great deal of your job will be performing routine but tedious tasks. This morning, you repair a sound-powered telephone.

✓ **Be a jack-of-all-trades.** You stand watch in the engine room to gain broad experience in all aspects of engineering. However, you're called on to emergency-troubleshoot a glitch in the aircraft landing/takeoff equipment. As the only electrical specialist on board, you're often expected to handle very complex tasks such as this one.

✓ **Work with civilian technical assistants.** In the afternoon, you shift gears to work with technically advanced equipment such as the glide slope indicator and the gyro compasses. You brainstorm solutions with civilian technical assistants—an outstanding training and educational experience.

What You Can Do Now

✴ Take relevant high school courses. Helpful school subjects include math, electricity and electronics, and shop mechanics.

✴ Enroll in a course at a community college. Taking classes demonstrates your interest and seriousness. It will also help you get your requested speciality.

✴ Work as a helper. You can learn many electrical skills this way. A helper assists electricians in setting up job sites, gathering materials, and doing other nonelectrical work. Look up opportunities on area job boards and ask around.

✴ Get into an apprenticeship program. This is not easy to do—and if you can do it, you may not want to join the military. However, this is the time-honored way to learn electrical skills.

The Inside Scoop: Q&A

Kim Fry
Electronics repair technician
Norfolk Naval Shipyard, Norfolk, Virginia

Q: *How did you get your job?*

A: When I first graduated from high school, I had never considered joining the military. I wanted to get out the house, get a job, and go to college. After [two years of] struggling to pay rent and tuition, I . . . decided to enter the navy—in a technical field, because I liked the educational options that went along with enlistment. I also knew technical skills would be in demand after I left the military. After some initial training, I had the opportunity to specialize in the electronics field. I decided to become an electronics technician because the big companies are always looking for those people.

Q: *What do you like best about your job?*

A: I . . . was impressed by the amount of preparation I received for my first tour . . . [It] was an unbelievable experience. I'm planning to finish college using the navy's tuition assistance programs, and I hope to become an officer one day.

Q: *What's the most challenging part of your job?*

A: [When I was] aboard the USS *Puget Sound* in the Mediterranean Sea, I repaired calibration and test equipment that was used to analyze the electronic components and systems on the ship, such as communications, radar and sonar, navigation, and electronic warfare systems . . . On the USS *Wasp*, I was responsible for insuring that the electronic systems were operating properly before the ship went on an extended cruise.

Q: *What are the key to success to being an electronics repair technician?*

A: Aboard ship—everybody must become a jack-of-all-trades!

What Training You'll Need

Job training for an electrical equipment repairer in the armed forces consists of nine weeks of basic training in which you will learn basic soldiering skills. If you successfully complete basic training, there are another 6 to 26 weeks of advanced individual training. Part of this training will take place in the classroom and part in on-the-job training. The amount of training you will receive depends on your specialty.

In the classroom, you will cover basic electrical system maintenance and repair procedures. This includes topics such as the basic principles of electricity and electronics, electrical circuit troubleshooting, soldering techniques, and the proper procedure for wiring switches, outlets, and junction boxes. Of course, you will also study safety procedures in some detail.

In the field, you will work with an experienced electrician to practice the installation and repair of electrical wiring systems and electrical products. At first, you will just drill holes, set anchors, and attach wiring. Later, you'll install, connect, and test wiring, outlets, and switches. Finally, you will learn techniques to troubleshoot communications systems and to install, maintain, and repair sophisticated computerized equipment.

Your training in the U.S. armed forces will teach you more than just electrical repair. More important, you will learn teamwork skills and attention to detail. The training you will receive in this field can often be used toward a bachelor's or associate's degree. You may also receive an opportunity for continued education through various military college programs, in addition to tuition assistance.

How to Talk Like a Pro

Here are a few words you'll hear in this career:

- ⚡ **Ape** Slang for an "auxiliary power unit" (or APU). This is a small turbine engine on an aircraft that is started with a battery. It then supplies electrical power for starting the main engines.
- ⚡ **GFCI** or **GFI** An abbreviation for "ground fault circuit interrupter." This is a type of circuit protection usually required in kitchens and bathrooms. It helps safeguard against shocks.
- ⚡ **Twidget** Nickname for a sailor in the electrical field.
- ⚡ **Uninterruptible Power Supply (UPS)** A UPS device provides a constant supply of power even if there are interruptions to the normal power supply. It is usually used with computer equipment.

How to Find a Job

Many young men and women enlist in the armed forces right out of high school. If you're 18 years old, all you have to do is visit a local recruiting office. Seventeen-year-olds can also enlist but need a parent's permission.

To serve in the U.S. military, a person must pass physical requirements and a background check. Academically, an applicant must score at least a 31 on the Armed Forces Qualification Test (AFQT). For the army, your service obligations would be determined at the recruiter's office. (Read the fine print carefully to understand what your possible length of service or number of tours.)

Secrets for Success

See the following suggestions and turn to the appendix for advice on résumés and interviews.

- Develop your troubleshooting skills. To be an electrical equipment repairer, it helps to be able to read blueprints, wiring plans, and repair orders. That's one of the main ways to determine what went wrong with a piece of electrical equipment and how to fix it.
- Listen to what people are saying. Sometimes the user of a machine may know more about its behavior than you think, and may be able to offer useful clues to fixing it.

Reality Check

Electricity is unforgiving of mistakes. Electrical equipment repairers risk injury from electrical shock. Accidents are rare, but they do happen. For instance, in the civilian world, the position of electrical power line repairers is usually ranked in the top 10 of the most dangerous jobs in the United States.

Some Other Jobs to Think About

- Machinists. Machinists make, repair, and modify metal and nonmetal parts for engines and other types of machines.
- Mechanic. You can still work in the repair field as a mechanic. This job comes with a host of subspecialties such as aircraft, automobile, electronics, engine, refrigeration, hydroelectric, and radio.

✯ Technical writer. If you like the field but do not want to climb the ladders, then this is a good option. You can write or rewrite complex scientific, training, or other professional material for a knowledgeable audience.

How You Can Move Up

✯ Advance in the military. In the armed forces, promotions can come quickly, based on time in service and merit. Some jobs within this field offer accelerated promotions to higher pay grades. After four years, you can become a senior repairer, the professional who manages the most complex repair jobs and helps less experienced repairers. After 18 years, you can rise to the level of maintenance superintendent. In this position, you would direct an entire repair facility.

✯ Advance in civilian life. Electricians usually advance to higher positions based on a combination of experience and extra coursework and passing licensing exams. The National Electrical Code, methods of installation, and the variety of materials are constantly changing. Sometimes, developing a specialty in a field such as low-voltage voice, data, and video systems can be a ticket to higher paying work. Experienced electricians with enthusiasm and leadership skills can advance to higher-paying positions as supervisors, project managers, construction superintendents, or contractors. They can also open their own business or become electrical inspectors.

Web Sites to Surf

Careers in the Military. This Web site is the starting point for any investigation of jobs in the armed forces. It includes many useful job descriptions and links. http://www.careersinthemilitary.com

Today's Military. This site gives in-depth information on each branch of the U.S. armed forces. http://www.todaysmilitary.com

International Brotherhood of Electrical Workers. The brotherhood represents about 750,000 electrical workers in a wide variety of fields. This large Web site is a gold mine for information on a career in electrical repair. http://www.ibew.org

Install and maintain computer systems

Computer Systems Specialist

Work with cutting-edge hardware and software

Troubleshoot and repair broken equipment

Computer Systems Specialist

If you love computers and want to work with some of the most sophisticated hardware and software available in the world, then a computer systems specialty may be the job for you. The U.S. armed forces is one of the world's largest computer users. The military uses computers to operate equipment during combat and for countless non-combat situations. Computers also manage personnel, logistics, communications, weather systems, and financial information. Computer systems specialists install, operate, and maintain the military's high-tech systems. These, in turn, allow the modern U.S. armed forces to function.

Is This Job for You?

Would working as a computer systems specialist be a good fit for you? To find out, read each of the following questions and answer "Yes" or "No."

Yes	No	**1.**	Are you interested in computer and telephone systems?
Yes	No	**2.**	Do you pride yourself on attention to detail?
Yes	No	**3.**	Can you understand and apply math concepts?
Yes	No	**4.**	Do you consider yourself responsible and mature?
Yes	No	**5.**	Can you be trusted with classified information?
Yes	No	**6.**	Would you enjoy working with multimillion dollar technical systems?
Yes	No	**7.**	Do you have good communication skills?
Yes	No	**8.**	Are you interested in solving puzzles and problems?
Yes	No	**9.**	Do you like work that requires attention to detail?
Yes	No	**10.**	Are you well organized?

If you answered "Yes" to most of these questions, you might consider a career as a computer systems specialist. To find out more about this job, read on.

What You'll Do

The job description of computer systems specialists is simple: to maintain, operate, and repair computer equipment. However, there is

Let's Talk Money

The federal government pay scale starts low and ends low but includes excellent benefits. Base salary is no more than $20,000 for the first three years. Military benefits include tuition support and health and life insurance. If you qualify as a computer systems specialist, you may be eligible for up to a $40,000 enlistment bonus. Civilian computer systems analysts have median annual earnings of are about $72,230, according 2006 data from the U.S. Bureau of Labor Statistics.

much more to this field than this streamlined explanation implies. Your most basic duties would be to work on hardware and software installation and maintenance. You would use computers to write programs and collect, enter, and process information. You would also plan, install, and maintain local area networks and wide area networks (LANs and WANs).

Working as a computer systems specialist is extremely challenging. You would probably work on a wide variety of state-of-the-art computers, from laptops to mainframes, developing, testing, and debugging computer programs.

If a computer system or network breaks down, it could be your job to troubleshoot and repair broken equipment. Once a system is working, you might have to perform preventive and corrective maintenance to make sure it stays running. You might also become expert at setting up and taking down computer equipment under field conditions. This might involve working under stress or extreme climate conditions while under enemy fire. You would be working with computers, but you would also be part of the military, so the job could be dangerous.

Computer systems specialists also perform military-specific duties. You might be assigned to detect enemy radar signals and determine their origin. You also might track inbound threats such as missiles, or operate underwater or satellite telecommunication systems. In many cases, you'd work with highly classified and coded information.

Each branch of the service has its own specific needs. For example, if you work with navy computers, you might have to identify and differentiate sounds produced by ships, submarines, torpedoes, sonar transmissions, marine life, and natural sounds. The job of a computer systems specialist is both wide-ranging and challenging.

Let's Talk Trends

Computers help run the modern world. Any training in this field is almost certain to result in a good job. There is a huge demand for people with computer expertise. As a computer systems specialist, you should be able to easily find a position you like in high-tech industry in or out of the military. The Bureau of Labor Statistics estimates that the employment of computer systems analysts is expected to grow much faster than average for all occupations through 2014.

Who **You'll Work For**

★ The four major branches. The army, navy, air force, and Marine Corps all use computer systems specialists.

★ The coast guard. Computer systems specialists are stationed throughout the coast guard, including in Alaska and Hawaii. They work out of large and small shops, shore unit stations, and on all major coast guard cutters.

Where **You'll Work**

Military computer systems specialists work in offices, laboratories, and computer sites on military bases or aboard ships. You'll usually perform your job in comfortable surroundings and won't have to worry about working outside in the rain. However, you will probably have to sit at a desk for hours at a time. Like other people who spend long periods in front of a computer terminal, computer systems specialists may develop eyestrain, backaches, headaches, and hand and wrist problems such as carpal tunnel syndrome. These are typical injuries for office workers.

Military computer systems specialists typically work about 40 hours a week, the same as many of their peers in civilian life. However, you may have to work longer hours, nights, or weekends in order to meet deadlines, solve specific problems, or help during large-scale military operations.

In some cases, your job could be done from remote locations using laptops, modems, e-mail, and the Internet. However, in most cases you'll probably have to travel on-site to install the system or fix the problem.

The Inside Scoop: Q&A

Dorothy Hartsfield
Computer emergency response team
Information Systems Command, Fort Belvoir, Virginia

Q: *How did you get your job as a computer systems specialist?*

A: I decided to specialize in computers after six years as an administrative staff member in the army. I switched specialty areas because I saw a great deal of opportunity for people with computer expertise. After my initial training, I performed systems analysis and troubleshooting duties for a financial system at the army's Information Systems Command. I was then posted to Fort Lee, Virginia, where I installed a complex contracting system that would be used at bases all over the world.

Q: *What do you like best about your job?*

A: [For me, working] on a team installing and maintaining a global command and control system. It was an exciting and hectic time because our mission was to do whatever it took to get the system online.

Q: *What's the most challenging part of your job?*

A: [It's responding quickly] to computer failures due to everything from natural disasters to intrusions by hackers. I maintain team readiness and ensure that the staff is well-trained on the latest technologies.

Q: *What are the keys to success to being a computer systems specialist?*

A: Teamwork skills . . . [because some projects require you to] work with personnel from all branches of the armed forces.

Your Typical Day

Here are some highlights for a typical day as a computer systems specialist for the navy.

✔ **Help install a system.** A new aircraft carrier has been commissioned for the navy. You're in charge of setting up network administration services such as e-mail accounts, user training, security, and virus protection.

✔ **Attend a meeting.** Formal and informal get-togethers are common. You might confer about how the navy can use the latest developments in computer software or perhaps discuss ways to defend against hackers.

✔ **Fix a breakdown.** The computers that control the navigation system aren't working. Is it a hardware or software problem? A virus? Figure it out and fix it—fast!

What You Can Do Now

⚡ Take relevant classes in high school. Helpful school subjects include computer science, math, and keyboarding.

⚡ Experiment with your own computer. There is no substitute for hands-on experience. You have to like playing around with computers to get involved in this field.

⚡ Get some experience. There are all sorts of jobs for people with computer skills. Any practical experience or previous training in telephone or computer systems maintenance and repair will help you break into this specialty.

What Training You'll Need

Job training for a computer systems specialist in the armed forces consists of about nine weeks of basic training during which you will learn basic soldiering skills. That is followed by 10 to 25 weeks of broad classroom instruction in the operation, maintenance, and repair of computers. You will study computer concepts as well as planning, designing, and testing computer systems. Classroom training includes instruction on computer processors, power supplies, disk and magnetic tape drives, network systems, displays, and printers. You will focus on how each item operates and develop troubleshooting techniques. The length of your job training depends on the specialty area.

You will also receive further on-the-job training and advanced courses in specific computer systems and current programming languages. Because security is so important to the military, an important part of your training will cover computer security issues, coding, and debugging. Working with computers is one of the most security-sensitive jobs in the entire armed forces.

As a computer systems specialist, you will also need a great deal of knowledge of electrical theory. Computer systems specialists sometimes have the responsibility to manage, repair, maintain, and install telephone systems and network cabling.

Most of the training in this field qualifies for college credit. You may be able to continue your education through various college programs and a variety of tuition assistance programs. Advanced training may also be available through classes offered by the armed forces.

How to Talk Like a Pro

Here are a few words you'll hear in this career:

* ✴ **Bandwidth** A system's information-carrying capacity.
* ✴ **Network** Two or more computers linked together, either by wires or by wireless routers, so that they can share information.
* ✴ **LAN** and **WAN** A local area network (LAN) is a computer network that connects a group of computers over a small area. A wide area network (WAN) covers a larger geographic area and may consist of LANs.
* ✴ **Remote manageability** A term that describes the ability to administer a networked computer without physically touching the computer.

How to Find a Job

Many young men and women enlist in the U.S. armed forces right out of high school. If you're 18 years old, you can simply sign up. At 17, you need a parent's permission.

To serve in the U.S. military, a person must pass physical requirements and a background check. Academically, an applicant must score at least a 31 on the Armed Forces Qualification Test (AFQT). For the army, your service obligations would be determined at the recruiter's office. You can be signed up to serve from two to five years. In the In the Marine Corps, the initial time commitment is four to six years. (Read the fine print of your service contract carefully before you agree to sign anything to understand your possible length or service and number of tours.)

In the civilian world, people with good computer skills are in enormous demand. However, hardware and software change so quickly in this field that it is crucial to keep up with the latest innovations. This may require taking a few classes at the local technical college or getting an advanced degree. When working with computers, knowledge truly is power, and it keeps you marketable in the civilian world.

Secrets for Success

See the following suggestions and turn to the appendix for advice on résumés and interviews.

- ✴ Good communications skills. You may have a tech job, but getting along with people remains a key component of your work. Grumpy or surly computer technicians, analysts, or managers rarely flourish in the field.
- ✴ Sometimes the customer is right! Just because you know more about computers doesn't mean you know more about the individual characteristics of particular systems you will be called upon to fix and maintain. Your colleagues' needs are what you are trying to meet.

Reality Check

As a computer systems specialist, you may spend many of your working hours communicating with people who have no idea what you're talking about. You have to be constantly willing to enlighten the less-technically adept without getting frustrated or losing your temper.

Some Other Jobs to Think About

- ✴ Computer operator or programmer, or systems administrator. Each military branch has a wide variety of subspecialties or other job classifications that include working with computers.
- ✴ Engineering technician. Workers in engineering also use computers extensively. Engineering technicians use scientific knowledge to solve an endless series of practical problems in areas as diverse as industry, the environment, electronics, and aerospace.
- ✴ Data entry. Want to work with computers without all that training? Data entry is an entry-level job for many people and often

serves as a stepping-stone to higher-paying jobs with increased responsibilities.

How You Can Move Up

✸ Advance in the military. In the armed services, promotions can come quickly, based on time in service and merit. After four years, you can become a senior computer systems specialist. In addition to handling other duties, these officers design and implement complex hardware and software programs for military organizations. They also test and debug computer systems. After 18 years, you can advance as high as computer systems operations supervisor. These officers manage entire computer centers.

✸ Advance in civilian life. Systems analysts can be promoted to senior or lead systems analyst. If you show you have leadership skills, you can become a project manager or advance into a management position. Specialized knowledge can be particularly useful if you plan on working as an independent consultant or opening your own firm. Working with computers is very results-driven; a successful career combines considerable experience with the most up-to-date knowledge.

Web Sites to Surf

Careers in the Military. This Web site is the starting point for any investigation of jobs in the armed forces. It includes many useful job descriptions and links. http://www.careersinthemilitary.com

Today's Military. This site gives in-depth information on each branch of the U.S. armed forces. http://www.todaysmilitary.com

USENIX—The Advanced Computing Systems Association. Since 1975, the association—whose name comes from "Unix users group"—has brought together computer engineers, system administrators, scientists, and technicians working on the cutting edge of the computing world. http://www.usenix.org

Association for Computing Machinery. The association delivers resources that advance computing as a science and a profession, and the Web site has a digital library as well as helpful publications, conferences, and career resources. http://www.acm.org

Provide care during emergencies

Medical Service Technician

Help prevent and treat diseases and injuries

Perform under life-and-death pressure

Medical Service Technician

Medical service technicians help keep the members of the U.S. armed forces fit for duty. They also provide medical care in critical situations. Physicians are not always immediately available to treat the injured or wounded in during combat or other emergencies. In these cases, medical service technicians provide basic treatment and help care for sick and wounded service members. People's lives can depend on the quick reactions and effective care of medical service technicians. It is a career that offers the opportunity to help others.

Is This Job for You?

Would working as a medical service technician be a good fit for you? To find out, read each of the following questions and answer "Yes" or "No."

Yes	No	1.	Are you motivated to help other people?
Yes	No	2.	Can you communicate effectively?
Yes	No	3.	Can you work under highly stressful conditions?
Yes	No	4.	Are you interested in the sciences?
Yes	No	5.	Are you detail-oriented?
Yes	No	6.	Are you willing to work in life-and-death situations?
Yes	No	7.	Are you patient?
Yes	No	8.	Are you sensitive to the needs of other people?
Yes	No	9.	Are you willing to take care of someone else's physical needs?
Yes	No	10.	Do you have a friendly manner?

If you answered "Yes" to most of these questions, you might consider a career as a medical service technician. To find out more about this job, read on.

What You'll Do

As a medical service technician, you would keep service members healthy and return them to health if they become sick or injured. Sometimes, these two roles involve the same procedures. The job entails both routine and emergency medical duties.

Let's Talk Money

Personnel with one to three years of service in the armed forces earn from $16,000 to $20,000 per year in base salary. Benefits—including health care, tuition support, career training, and life insurance—are excellent. Active-duty service people receive many other benefits. In civilian life, an emergency medical technician (EMT) is a comparable job to a medical service technician. According to 2006 data from the U.S. Bureau of Labor Statistics, the annual mean salary for EMTs is $29,390.

On the routine side, medical service technicians help examine and treat patients who have minor injuries or common diseases. You would take the patient's temperature, pulse, and blood pressure, as well as collect blood samples, record test results, operate X-ray equipment, and change bandages and dressings. Technicians also prepare operating rooms, equipment, and supplies for surgery and perform some preoperative and postoperative care. You may also give shots and medicines to patients.

The job also has an administrative component. It is the medical service technician's job to interview patients, record their medical histories, and maintain treatment records. You might also be assigned to keep health records and clinical files up to date.

During wartime, you would assist physicians and dentists with emergency medical treatment. Injured or wounded service members need immediate treatment. When physicians are not readily available, you would be authorized to step in to provide basic medical or dental treatment to battlefield casualties. In this role, you would perform medical procedures, suture wounds, and apply casts to broken limbs. In special circumstances, you might even administer substances such as nitroglycerin, glucose, epinephrine, and albuterol. In the field, a medical service technician is a sort of jack-of-all-trades of medical care.

In guerilla-type wars such as the second Gulf War in Iraq, medics sometimes ride along on patrols to care for injuries if necessary. In such situations, you would be wearing body armor and a helmet and carrying your weapons at all times. This type of warfare can be scary because U.S. soldiers often do not know the identity of the enemy, and attacks can come at any time. For example, there were more than 10,000 roadside bombings in Iraq in 2005. Wartime injuries can be particularly bloody and traumatic compared with the typical emergencies in the United States. As a medical service technician, you would need to prepare to help fellow recruits under possibly harrowing conditions.

Who You'll Work For

✷ The army, navy, air force, and coast guard. The navy handles medical services for the Marine Corps.

✷ Medcom. The U.S. Army Medical Command, headquartered in San Antonio, Texas, provides peacetime medical care to a patient population of more than three million people. It also conducts training, and plans and maintains readiness for wartime health care operations.

✷ A military hospital. For example, Walter Reed Army Medical Center, in Washington, D.C., serves more than 150,000 active and retired personnel from all branches of the military.

Where You'll Work

Medical service technicians usually work in hospitals and clinics. These might be in combat zones, at military bases, or aboard ships or submarines. The job requires a great deal of bending, kneeling, and heavy lifting. Pulled muscles are a common ailment. Post-traumatic stress disorder (PTSD) is also a possibility for people new to working in health care. Many medical service technicians have prior experience working with gunshot wounds and car wrecks, but even they sometimes have trouble coping with the random violence.

Let's Talk Trends

As long as people need medical and dental services, medical service technicians will be in demand. The military offers an opportunity for high school graduates to get training and experience in the medical and dental professions. In civilian life, emergency medical technicians and paramedics held about 200,000 jobs in 2007. The number is expected to grow rapidly over the next 10 years, according to the Bureau of Labor Statistics.

Medical service technicians may give emergency medical treatment in the field. In a combat area, such as in Iraq or Afghanistan, you may find yourself accompanying patrols or helping in transporting the wounded in dangerous situations. Medical service technicians deal with the same sorts of situations that EMTs do in the United States except that, in the field, they may see a lot more physical trauma. In a battlefield situation, for instance, you may have to treat abdominal, head, and chest wounds.

Sometimes medical technicians work standard hours assisting with outpatient and inpatient care and treatment. However, emergency services function 24 hours a day, and hospitals can't close for Christmas or the Fourth of July. This means you may have to work irregular working hours.

Your Typical Day

Here are some highlights for a typical day as a medical service technician.

✔ **Vaccinate service members.** This morning, you will help to vaccinate recruits against measles, mumps, and rubella (MMR), regardless of their prior history. You'll help organize the flow of work, assist the administering physician and nurse, and may help give the shots.

✔ **Prepare the operating room for surgery.** You'll make sure there are sufficient operating rooms, equipment, and supplies for all surgeries scheduled in the afternoon. If supplies are low, you'll order them.

✔ **Provide emergency medical care.** A solider has choked on a chicken bone at dinner. You look for ABC: airway, breathing, and circulation. He's not breathing, so you do intubation (place a tube down the throat and into the windpipe). There's no pulse, so you do cardiopulmonary resuscitation (CPR). The soldier is alive, but full recovery is uncertain. Accidents happen every day in a population as large as that of the armed services.

What You Can Do Now

✰ Take relevant high school classes. Good subject choices include chemistry, biology, psychology, math, and general science.

The Inside Scoop: Q&A

Roger Buck
Chief petty officer
Naval Training Station, Great Lakes, Illinois

Q: *How did you get your job?*

A: I always knew that I wanted to go into the medical profession. My mom has been ill throughout my life, so I spent a lot of time in hospitals while I was growing up. Plus, I like taking care of people. After navy boot camp, I trained to become a hospital corpsman. Then, I received specialized training at the Field Medical Service School (FMSS) in Camp LeJeune, North Carolina, to learn how to handle field and trauma medicine with marines.

Q: *What do you like best about your job?*

A: I have had many great experiences. Recently, I was stationed for several months in Umm Qasr, a port in southern Iraq. There, I was . . . training the Iraqi navy and marines on various medical platforms, and I oversaw the building and staffing of a medical clinic.

Q: *What's the most challenging part of your job?*

A: Once trained, you are responsible for the treatment of every medical condition imaginable—from arm fractures to appendicitis to heart attacks. So, when I was deployed on a fast-attack nuclear-powered submarine, I had to make sure that the sailors were healthy, both physically and mentally, especially because submarines can be at sea for long periods at a time. I gave immunizations, counseled the sailors, and monitored the radiation levels of all personnel on board due to their exposure to nuclear power.

Q: *What are the keys to success to being a medical service technician?*

A: [Providing] the best possible care to new recruits.

✦ Take a specialized course. Many community colleges, technical schools, universities, and fire and police academies offer emergency medical training.

✦ Become a first responder. This is an excellent way to acquire experience. Requirements for first responders vary from state to state. In general, it takes about 40 hours of training over about two months. If you cannot do this, at least volunteer at a hospital or trauma center.

What Training You'll Need

Job training for a medical service technician in the armed forces consists of about nine weeks of basic training. This is followed by as few as seven or as many as 52 weeks of advanced training in the classroom and in the field. The amount of training depends on your specialty.

In classes, you will study the human body and biology in some detail and then learn basic nursing care. Your instructors will also cover wide-ranging topics such as surgical and laboratory procedures, diagnosing diseases, sterilizing surgical equipment, and plaster-casting techniques.

Medical service technicians play an important part in medical care on the battlefield. Because of this, some of your training will focus on recognizing and treating life-threatening emergencies outside the hospital environment. You'll receive instruction and practice in dealing with medical emergencies such as bleeding, fractures, cardiac arrest, seizures, and airway obstruction. You'll also learn how to manage serious injuries such as falls, fractures, cuts, and burns. All this training also requires you to know how to use emergency equipment such as backboards, suction devices, splints, oxygen delivery systems, and stretchers. Medical service technicians must also be proficient in CPR.

Further medical training occurs as you gain experience in your position. You can also take advanced courses. Some technicians may specialize in fields such as radiology, search and rescue, and preventive medicine

Most of your training in the medical and dental fields can be applied for credit at colleges and universities. With study and experience, you may qualify for certification with the National Registry of Emergency Medical Technicians (NREMT), a terrific résumé-builder that shows you have mastered the techniques of basic care.

How to Talk Like a Pro

Here are a few words you'll hear in this career:

* **Debridement** The cleaning of an open wound by removing dead tissue and foreign material. Debridement of burns is extremely painful.
* **Myocardial infarction** A heart attack.
* **Sepsis** A very severe infection.
* **Thrombosis** A blood clot.
* **Venipuncture** The drawing of blood from a vein.

How to Find a Job

Many young men and women enlist in the armed forces right out of high school. Eighteen-year-olds can do so on their own; 17-year-olds can enlist with a parent's permission.

To serve in the U.S. military, a person must pass physical requirements and a background check. Academically, an applicant must score at least a 31 on the Armed Forces Qualification Test (AFQT). For the army, your service obligations would be determined at the recruiter's office. You can agree with the recruiter to serve for two, three, four, or even five years.

In civilian life, private ambulance services or hospitals advertise medical service jobs on the Internet and in newspapers. Job openings are sometimes posted by local governments for work in fire departments, public ambulance services, and emergency medical services.

Secrets for Success

See the following suggestions and turn to the appendix for advice on résumés and interviews.

* Keep calm and be personable. Even routine medical care will make some patients nervous. Your job will be much easier if you remain calm and friendly.
* Learn from those around you. The practical lessons of doing medical work under sometimes-stressful circumstances will be many. If you steadily build on and improve your techniques, you may go far in the field of medicine.

Reality Check

This job is not for the faint at heart or the easily depressed. There can be a lot of blood and gore, and the work is physically strenuous. In addition, dealing with life-or-death situations and suffering or dying patients can be extremely stressful.

Some Other Jobs to Think About

☆ Military possibilities. In the armed forces, other comparable careers include operating room specialist, preventative medicine specialist, radiology specialist, and respiratory specialist. These jobs all require quick and level-headed reactions to life-or-death situations.

☆ Civilian possibilities. Emergency medical technicians treat victims of accidents, fire, or heart attacks. Medical assistants work for physicians and perform routine medical and clerical tasks. Medication aides give shots and medicine under the supervision of physicians. Physician assistants perform routine examinations and treatment for physicians.

How You Can Move Up

☆ Advance in the military. In the armed forces promotions can come quickly, based on time in service and merit. After several years, medical service technicians can advance into supervisory positions. After 18 years, you can advance as high as medical services coordinator. These officers oversee training, health care, and disaster control programs.

☆ Advance in civilian life. In civilian life, emergency medical training is offered at progressive levels: EMT-1 (basic), EMT-2 (intermediate), EMT-3, and EMT-4 (paramedic). To advance in this career requires progressively harder coursework as well as clinical and field experience. Advancement beyond the paramedic level usually means leaving fieldwork completely to become a supervisor, operations manager, or executive director of emergency services. If you like the health care field, you can return to school and become a registered nurse, physician, or other health care worker.

Web Sites to Surf

Careers in the Military. This Web site is the starting point for any investigation of jobs in the armed forces. It includes many useful job descriptions and links. http://www.careersinthemilitary.com

Today's Military. This site gives in-depth information on each branch of the U.S. armed forces. http://www.todaysmilitary.com

National Association of Emergency Medical Technicians (NAEMT). The NAEMT, founded in 1975, is the nation's largest and oldest organization representing EMTs and paramedics. This Web site has information about educational programs and research and many useful links. http://www.naemt.org

Provide career counseling

Personnel Specialist

Analyze, process, and maintain confidential files

Learn office-management skills

Personnel Specialist

What do you want to do for your career? If you're reading this book, then you're not entirely sure of the answer. That's okay; most people aren't. That is where personnel specialists come in. They help other people make career choices by providing advice and direction. The U.S. armed forces has more than one million service members and hundreds of job specialties. The military needs to recruit top-quality people and assign them to positions in which they will excel. It is the job of personnel specialists to help fit the right person with the right job. Personnel specialists also provide counseling and career guidance for service members once they join the armed forces. Personnel specialists have the knowledge to shape the careers and the lives of members of the military and their families.

Is This Job for You?

Would working as a personnel specialist be a good fit for you? To find out, read each of the following questions and answer "Yes" or "No."

Yes	No	**1.**	Do you like to work closely with other people?
Yes	No	**2.**	Can you communicate clear instructions and correspondence?
Yes	No	**3.**	Do you have good writing skills?
Yes	No	**4.**	Are you a good listener?
Yes	No	**5.**	Are you willing to sit at a desk all day?
Yes	No	**6.**	Can you follow detailed procedures and instructions?
Yes	No	**7.**	Are you interested in business administration?
Yes	No	**8.**	Do you have good computer and typing skills?
Yes	No	**9.**	Do you avoid making judgments based on appearance?
Yes	No	**10.**	Do you like math?

If you answered "Yes" to most of these questions, you might consider a career as a personnel specialist. To find out more about this job, read on.

Let's Talk Money

Compensation in the military is primarily based on years of service, and base salary does not rise above $20,000 until after three years of service. Government benefits are famously excellent and include career training, health care, some money for college, and life insurance. In civilian life, according to 2006 figures from the U.S. Bureau of Labor Statistics, human resource assistants averaged $34,700 a year; human resources specialists earned an average of $54,700 a year.

What You'll Do

Like most large organizations, the U.S. armed forces' most valuable resource is its people. Personnel specialists try to fill military positions with the most competent and qualified workers. Although personnel specialists sometimes are responsible for recruiting, their primary focus is placing and helping service members once they are already in the military.

As a personnel specialist, you would advise service members on career development, special assignments, training, and other personnel issues. You would offer individual counseling related to promotions, rights, and benefits. It would also be part of your job to provide legal and religious support, education, or even advice on personal problems and family matters. To do this, you would work directly with service personnel and their families and assist them in making decisions that affect their military life. The nice thing about the job is that you are helping others, whether it's at the career level, through day-to-day activities, or with their personal life.

Personnel specialists also perform administrative duties. They collect and manage information about the people in the military. This includes records on training, job assignments, promotions, and health information. Information of this nature needs to be well organized and properly documented. You would also maintain and review personnel information files and supporting documents both manually and by computer. You'd provide service members with guidance about rights and benefits, career and education counseling, and legal assistance. You would also help organize religious activities.

Working as a personnel specialist is all about assisting others. In this job, you will be helping service members fulfill their individual needs and goals.

Who You'll Work For

* ⭐ Army
* ⭐ Navy
* ⭐ Air force
* ⭐ Marine Corps
* ⭐ Coast guard

Where You'll Work

Personnel specialists normally work in offices. This might mean on land or aboard ships. You may be stationed at a base in the United States or you might be posted anywhere around the world. Personnel specialists are needed at almost any location where there are members of the U.S. armed forces.

Office work has its advantages and disadvantages. It means that you will usually work in clean and comfortable settings. Unlike electrical repair specialists, you will not be working at the mercy of the weather. The heat in Iraq or the cold in Greenland will not affect your work. On the other hand, you will have to sit at a desk for long periods, while you review data or interview people. Part of what will make your job satisfying will be your office colleagues.

One of your main tasks will be to maintain personnel, legal, and administrative records. Computers have made file cabinets almost obsolete. You will be doing a great deal of your work in front of a computer screen, writing letters, reports, and correspondence and entering data. You might experience eye and muscle strain, backaches, headaches, and repetitive motion injuries. These are not uncommon injuries for office workers.

Let's Talk Trends

Human resources departments are essential to organizations around the world today. Companies often list "people skills" as among the most desirable characteristics in their employees. The skills you develop in the military in the personnel field will remain extremely desirable to civilian employers. The Bureau of Labor Statistics estimates that the overall employment of human resources workers is expected to grow faster than the average for all occupations through 2014.

Personnel specialists usually work a regular schedule. Like their peers in the civilian work force, personnel specialists usually work 9 to 5 and a standard 40-hour week. There might be occasional periods during which you would have to work overtime, but these will probably be rare.

Your Typical Day

Here are some highlights for a typical day as a personnel specialist.

✔ **Enter and retrieve personnel information.** This morning you will be locating all the relevant career information for a general who is retiring to help her with her retirement package.

✔ **Process personnel action forms.** You will work your way through your to-do list, as you make sure the proper paperwork is filled out for a variety of promotions, awards, reassignments, retirements, reenlistments, separations (discharges), and reclassifications (changes in job specialties).

✔ **Provide career counseling.** It is your job to find the best possible career path for service members. This afternoon, you will be helping a sailor fresh out of basic training to find a job specialty. He is interested in weapons and electronics, so you think he might make a perfect weapons maintenance technician.

What Training You'll Need

In order to become a personnel specialist, you will receive both classroom schooling and on-the-job training. First, however, you will receive about two months of basic training in which you will learn basic soldiering skills. This will be followed by about two more months of advanced training. In the classroom, you will learn the proper preparation of military correspondence, the management of personnel records, and computer skills. Instructors will also help you to brush up your knowledge of general office skills and basic keyboarding.

Learning U.S. armed forces forms can be a daunting task. The military is a large bureaucratic organization. There are hundreds of forms covering what seems to be every imaginable contingency. It is your job to know which form is required, how to fill it out, and to whom to send it.

Your on-the-job training with an experienced personnel specialist is crucial. You'll learn to become an expert with logs, records, reports,

The Inside Scoop: Q&A

Howard Miranda
Personnel specialist, customer service
Bolling Air Force Base, Washington, D.C.

Q: *How did you get your job?*

A: I grew up in Chesapeake, Virginia, and . . . I enlisted in the air force in 2003 to try something new. I went to boot camp at Lackland Air Force Base in Texas. I went in "open general," which means that I hadn't chosen a career field. I wasn't sure what I wanted to do. Based on my strengths on the ASVAB [career-counseling] tests, I was directed to administrative-type work and chose the career field of "personnelist."

Q: *What do you like best about your job?*

A: After boot camp, I did my technical training, which consisted of learning clerical skills and also learning about the Air Force personnel regulations. I was very lucky when I got my first duty assignment. I was able to go to Okinawa. This was a great experience. I learned some Japanese and also learned how the Japanese live.

Q: *What's the most challenging part of your job?*

A: At the air base in Okinawa, I worked in personnel readiness. Our office was accountable for all personnel who were deployed from the air base. We cut the deployment orders and also kept track of everyone who was deployed. Because we were deploying our people to Iraq and Qatar, we had to coordinate with several office skills.

Q: *What are the keys to success to being a personnel specialist?*

A: [One key is learning] how to become an effective public speaker. Before I joined the military, I was not good at speaking in front of people and did not like it at all. Now, I help coordinate the Right Start orientations on base, which every newcomer needs to attend. I speak in front of large groups on a regular basis and I've become really comfortable with it.

and computer programs. Someone with experience can teach you which shortcuts can and cannot be used in filling out paperwork. Like most jobs, actual personnel work in the field differs considerably from how it is described in books.

Advanced training is also available to you during later stages of your career. In addition, you can use the skills you learn in the personnel field to acquire semester credit hours for a vocational certificate as well as a bachelor's or associate's degree.

How to Talk Like a Pro

Here are a few words you'll hear in this career:

* **Benefits** The military provides a package of non-monetary compensation in addition to the base salary of service members. It includes health insurance, life insurance, disability insurance, tuition assistance, and several others extras.
* **DD 4** Enlistment or reenlistment document.
* **DS3** Abbreviation for "Disabled Soldier Support System." The U.S. Army will provide severely disabled soldiers and their families with help as they transition from active military service to their civilian communities.
* **HR** An abbreviation for "human resources." HR denotes people who staff and operate an organization—as opposed to the financial and material resources of an organization.
* **I-9** Employment Eligibility Verification Form that is required by the Department of Homeland Security to document eligibility for employment in the United States.

How to Find a Job

Many young men and women enlist in the armed forces right out of high school. Eighteen-year-olds can do so on their own; if you're 17, you need a parent's permission.

To serve in the U.S. military, a person must pass physical requirements and a background check. Academically, an applicant must score at least a 31 on the Armed Forces Qualification Test (AFQT). For most branches, your service obligations would be determined at the recruiter's office. You can agree with the recruiter to serve for two, three, four, or even five years. Job specialties are also negotiable.

(Read the fine print of your service contract carefully to understand your possible length of service and number of tours of duty.)

In civilian life, you can get information about working in personnel or human resources departments from newspapers, the Internet, or employment agencies. As always, however, personal knowledge of the job opening or inside information is usually more effective in getting the job you want.

Secrets for Success

See the following suggestions and turn to the appendix for advice on résumés and interviews.

* Have great people skills. Personnel specialists analyze, process, and maintain information files. However, they also deal with human beings. The trick is to treat each service member not as a "case," but as an individual with hopes and dreams.
* Be organized. It's a skill you develop and not just a personality trait. Without the ability to quickly find what you need it's impossible to give people the help you want to give them.

Reality Check

You may be in the military, but a position in human resources is an administrative one. You'll use word processing, spreadsheets, and databases. If you want to hone these skills, ask yourself: Why join when you can get the same job in the civilian world for less commitment and more money?

Some Other Jobs to Think About

* Paralegal. Paralegals use their education, experience, and training to perform some of the same tasks as lawyers.
* Office manager. An office manager might be a secretary, receptionist, bookkeeper, or technology troubleshooter. They often handle some work similar to the personnel specialist such as filing, bookkeeping, and human resources.
* Career counselor. This job focuses on one aspect of personnel work. Career counselors serve as advisors to their clients. They help people examine their interests and abilities to pinpoint the profession that best suits them.

How You Can Move Up

★ Advance in the military. In the armed forces, promotions can come quickly, based on time in service and merit. In this field, you can advance as high as personnel supervisor. Supervisors assign new personnel clerks and organize training programs.

★ Advance in civilian life. In civilian life, personnel specialists work for all types of organizations, including corporations, stores, and government agencies. Payroll, timekeeping, and human resources departments of most companies require the kinds of skills that you will acquire as a personnel specialist. The experience you get in the military will help open the door, but many civilian employers primarily promote personnel specialists who have taken college-level courses or have majored in human resources, human resources administration, or industrial and labor relations. A specific technical or business background might also help you receive a higher position in human resources.

Web Sites to Surf

Careers in the Military. This Web site is the starting point for any investigation of jobs in the armed forces. It includes many useful job descriptions and links. http://www.careersinthemilitary.com

Today's Military. This site gives in-depth information on each branch of the U.S. armed forces. http://www.todaysmilitary.com

National Human Resources Association. The association was established in 1951 to provide programs and services for human resource professionals. This site has good resources for members. http://www.humanresources.org

Keep equipment running

Machinist

Craft machine parts by hand

Solve mechanical problems

Machinist

Engines and machines can break down no matter how well they are maintained. The engines and machines of the U.S. armed forces are not any different. If the machines are expensive, someone has to repair broken parts, and sometimes, those parts are not available. In these cases, new parts must be made. This is the machinist's job. They perform incredibly accurate work—sometimes to within a margin of 1/10,000th of an inch—and so, require amazing concentration and physical effort. Without the intelligence and hard work of machinists, the high-tech equipment of the U.S. armed forces would turn into nothing more than a bunch of metal surrounded by wires.

Is This Job for You?

Would working as a machinist be a good fit for you? To find out, read each of the following questions and answer "Yes" or "No."

Yes	No	**1.**	Do you enjoy solving mechanical problems?
Yes	No	**2.**	Are you extremely detail-oriented?
Yes	No	**3.**	Do you like to work with your hands?
Yes	No	**4.**	Do you like to apply mathematical formulas?
Yes	No	**5.**	Can you concentrate in a noisy environment?
Yes	No	**6.**	Do you enjoy making things?
Yes	No	**7.**	Can you work independently?
Yes	No	**8.**	Do you like a job that requires physical effort?
Yes	No	**9.**	Do you enjoy a challenge?
Yes	No	**10.**	Are you willing to work standing up most of the day?

If you answered "Yes" to most of these questions, you might consider a career as a machinist. To find out more about this job, read on.

What You'll Do

As a machinist in the armed forces, you would make, repair, and modify metal and nonmetal parts for engines and other types of machines. You'd operate tools such as lathes, drill presses, grinders, shapers, hacksaws, band saws, and milling machines. You might be taught how to use all these machines or you might specialize in one or two. You'd then use your skill with machine tools to plan and make machined products that meet exact specifications.

Let's Talk Money

Salaries in the U.S. armed forces depend on performance and time in service. In general, a machinist with three years experience makes about $1,500 a month, or $18,000 a year, in addition to excellent benefits. In civilian life, according to 2006 data from the U.S. Bureau of Labor Statistics, machinists average about $17 an hour, or $35,810 per year.

The nature of the machinist's job is changing quickly. Many machinists today now use tools that are "computer numerically controlled," also known as CNC. In this case, you'd work with computer control programmers to decide how the automated equipment will cut a part. The programmer may choose the path of the cut while you would determine the type and speed of the cutting tool and the feed rate. Most machinists now train in CNC programming. They may write basic programs and then change the programs based on problems in test runs. Machinists may also operate the CNC machines themselves after the production process is designed.

Some precision machinists produce small batches or one-of-a-kind items. Others, known as production machinists, produce large quantities of one specific part. This process is almost completely automated and the machine tools operate without anyone present. One production machinist, working an eight-hour day, might check equipment, replace worn cutting tools, and perform other tasks on several CNC machines that operate 24 hours a day.

After the work is completed, machinists check the accuracy of their work against blueprints. They use tools such as micrometers, calipers, rulers, and depth gauges.

Modern production techniques require machinists to have a wide range of skills. Constantly working with million-dollar machinery and equipment carries a great deal of pressure. However, if you are technically oriented, have strong troubleshooting skills, and enjoy working with your hands, you might love the challenges of working as a machinist.

Who You'll Work For

* Army
* Navy

Let's Talk Trends

Machinists will always be needed because anything with gears, electronics, or wiring eventually breaks down. The armed services have about 2,300 machinists. On average, they need about 110 new machinists each year, so the competition for these jobs is stiff. In civilian life, machinists hold about 370,000 jobs. However, the Bureau of Labor Statistics projects that the employment of machinists will grow more slowly than the average for other occupations through at least 2014.

* Air force
* Marine Corps
* Coast guard

Where You'll Work

As a machinist in the military, you would enjoy better-than-average working conditions for this profession. Most machine shops in the U.S. armed forces are relatively clean, well lit, and ventilated. Machine shops can be noisy places, but many computer-controlled machines in military shops are partially or completely enclosed. This reduces the exposure of machinists to noise, dirt, and the lubricants used to cool workpieces during machining.

However, the job still requires stamina. Machinists stand most of the day and occasionally need to lift heavy workpieces. Many military machine shops try to reduce the problem of heavy lifting using autoloaders and overhead cranes. Most machinists work a 40-hour week. However, you may occasionally have to work evening and weekend shifts if the demand is urgent.

In civilian life, most machinists work in small machine shops or in manufacturing industries such as machinery manufacturing and transportation equipment manufacturing (for cars and planes). Maintenance machinists work in almost all industries that use any kind of production machinery.

Your Typical Day

Here are some highlights for a typical day as an armed forces machinist.

The Inside Scoop: Q&A

Nancy Tita
Staff sergeant
Aberdeen Proving Ground, Aberdeen, Maryland

Q: *How did you get your job as a machinist?*

A: I joined the Army Reserves for training so I could do something different from my civilian job as a clerk. . . . For a year, I worked several weekends a month with my reserve unit; then I volunteered for active duty, and I asked to receive training as a machinist. I thought the work would be challenging and different and would allow me to prove myself. I went through initial training [and] I learned the basic skills required of all machinists. I was able to learn my trade quickly and became familiar with some of the other occupations in the maintenance shop. . . . I [have also] supervised a crew that repaired jeeps, tanks, and other armored equipment.

Q: *What do you like best about your job?*

A: [I like] helping to make repairs to everything from radios to helicopters.

Q: *What is the most challenging part of your job?*

A: I was recently promoted to staff sergeant and look forward to being one of the top-ranking females in the maintenance field. I like the challenge of being the only female in the unit.

Q: *What are the keys to success to being a machinist?*

A: [Continue to] learn the latest technologies. And just have fun.

✔ **Review the blueprints.** Before you "machine" a part, you carefully plan and prepare the operation. Your job is to repair a broken part, so you study the electronic and written blueprints. You also examine the specifications for the job.

✔ **Make the calculations.** You calculate where to cut or bore into the workpiece and how fast to feed it into the machine. Then you choose the proper tools and materials for the job and finishing operations.

✔ **Machine the workpiece.** Finally, the prep work is completed. You position the workpiece on the machine tool, set the controls, and make the cuts. You constantly check the feed rate and speed of the machine and make sure the workpiece is being properly lubricated and cooled. The temperature of the workpiece is very important because most metals expand when heated. Machinists must consider temperature and adjust the size of their cuts.

What You Can Do Now

✴ Take relevant classes in high school. Helpful school subjects include mathematics (especially trigonometry), general science, metalworking, blueprint reading, drafting, and/or mechanical drawing.

✴ Get some experience. Any practical experience with machine tools would be extremely valuable. If possible, try to find an apprenticeship program for machine setters, operators, or tenders.

✴ Take a vocational course. Many machinists learn the trade through two-year associate's degree programs at community or technical colleges. Try a course in mechanics, machine shop, electricity, or practical math.

What Training You'll Need

Job training for a military machinist usually begins with nine weeks of basic training, in which you'll learn basic soldiering skills. This will be followed by about 14 weeks of advanced individual training, including practice in machine operation. Part of this time is spent in the classroom and part in on-the-job training. Classroom instruction includes math, physics, science, blueprint reading, mechanical drawing, quality control, and safety practices. Some other skills you'll learn include recognizing machine types; mastering their uses, setup, and operation; and learning the various qualities of different metals. In field training, an experienced machinist supervises apprentices while they learn how to operate various machine tools. The length and nature of your training depends on your job.

As machine shops have increased their use of computer-controlled equipment, training in the operation and programming of CNC machine tools has become essential. Engineers keep creating new types of machine tools and new materials to machine, so machinists must constantly receive extra training to update their skills. The military may provide this training, or a representative of the equipment manufacturer may provide it. In addition to operating machines that use metal cutting tools, machinists sometimes use machines that cut with lasers, water jets, or electrified wires. Though some of the computer controls may be similar, machinists must understand the unique cutting properties of these different machines.

Further training occurs on the job and through advanced courses. Some machinist's jobs offer accelerated promotions to higher pay grades. The training you would receive as a machinist may count as credit hours toward a bachelor's or associate's degree. You may also receive an opportunity for continued education through various armed forces college programs in addition to tuition assistance.

How to Talk Like a Pro

Here are a few words you'll hear in this career:

- ✬ **CNC machines** Abbreviation for "computer numerically controlled" machines. CNC machines follow a computer program that can control the cutting tool speed, change dull tools, and perform all of the necessary cuts to create a part.
- ✬ **Machine tool** A drill press, lathe, grinder, milling machine, or other type of machine, usually used to work metal.
- ✬ **Workpiece** The piece of steel, aluminum, titanium, plastic, silicon, or any other material that is being shaped.

How to Find a Job

Many young men and women enlist in the armed forces right out of high school. At 18 years old, you can enlist on your own; 17-year-olds need the permission of a parent.

To serve in the U.S. military, a person must pass physical requirements and a background check. Academically, an applicant must score at least a 31 on the Armed Forces Qualification Test (AFQT). For the army, your service obligations would be determined at the recruiter's office. You can agree with the recruiter to serve for two, three, four, or even five years. (Read the fine print of your service contract carefully before you agree to sign anything to understand your possible length or service and number of tours of duty.)

Secrets for Success

See the following suggestions and turn to the appendix for advice on résumés and interviews.

⭐ Good machinists work with their heads as much as their hands. An ability to read blueprints and apply mathematical formulas is indispensable. Most machinists now rely on computer-aided design (CAD) programs, so good computer skills are also crucial.

⭐ The old adage from carpentry is also appropriate in the work of a machinist: Measure twice, cut once. Pausing to check one's work is always a good idea.

Reality Check

Machinists may work far from battlefields, but this does not mean the job has no risks. Workers around machine tools need to wear protective equipment, such as safety glasses, to shield against bits of flying metal. They also spend many days using earplugs to dampen machinery noise. Handling hazardous coolants and lubricants requires caution. It's safer than being in the infantry, but not as safe a job as a finance and accounting specialist, for example.

Some Other Jobs to Think About

⭐ Tool and die maker. These highly skilled machinists produce tools, dies, and parts of machines used to manufacture a variety of products.

⭐ Welder. This job also requires precision and skill in working with metal.

⭐ Auto or truck mechanic. There's always a shortage of good transportation mechanics, especially as car engines become increasingly complex.

How You Can Move Up

⭐ Advance in the military. In the armed forces, promotions can come quickly, based on time in service and merit. After three years, you will become eligible to be a senior machinist. Among other duties, senior machinists perform difficult machine setup and operation for precision work. After 16 years, you can advance as high as a mechanical maintenance superintendent. These officers oversee all shop administration at a facility.

✸ Advance in civilian life. Civilian factories and repair shops in many industries, such as the electrical product, automotive, and heavy machinery industries, are always looking for experienced machinists. Experienced machinists may become CNC programmers or tool and die makers. It is also possible to be promoted to a supervisory position in a firm. Promotions usually depend on experience, job evaluations, and extra classroom training.

Web Sites to Surf

Careers in the Military. This Web site is the starting point for any investigation of jobs in the armed forces. It includes many useful job descriptions and links. http://www.careersinthemilitary.com

Today's Military. This site gives in-depth information on each branch of the U.S. armed forces. http://www.todaysmilitary.com

Precision Metalforming Association (PMA). The PMA Educational Foundation, established in 1996, is a good source for training information for this field. http://www.pma.org

International Association of Machinists and Aerospace Workers. The largest machinist's union contains a great deal of information of interest to anyone beginning this career. http://www.goiam.org

Protect lives and property

Law Enforcement and Security Specialist

Hold a position of respect and authority

Investigate crimes

Law Enforcement and Security Specialist

An officer fudges the books to steal money. Two soldiers get into a brutal fight over whose hometown team is better. Crimes occur in all large organizations; the U.S. military is no exception. Law enforcement and security specialists are the military's police officers. They investigate crimes committed on military property or those that involve service members of the U.S. armed forces.

Law enforcement and security specialists are also the armed forces' first line of defense. It is their job to maintain discipline on all military bases and installations. Military police protect lives and property by enforcing military rules and regulations. This is a career for you if you want to investigate accidents and crimes, prepare reports on the incidents, and arrest suspects when necessary.

Is This Job for You?

Would working as a law enforcement and security specialist be a good fit for you? To find out, read each of the following questions and answer "Yes" or "No."

Yes	*No*	**1.**	Can you work well independently and as a member of a team?
Yes	*No*	**2.**	Are you sensitive to others' feelings and needs?
Yes	*No*	**3.**	Are you willing to perform potentially dangerous work?
Yes	*No*	**4.**	Are you willing to work outdoors most of the day?
Yes	*No*	**5.**	Can you learn and apply rules, regulations, and laws?
Yes	*No*	**6.**	Do you believe in the importance of the law?
Yes	*No*	**7.**	Do you enjoy working with people?
Yes	*No*	**8.**	Are you honest, reliable, and responsible?
Yes	*No*	**9.**	Can you remain alert and calm in stressful situations?
Yes	*No*	**10.**	Can you think and react quickly?

If you answered "Yes" to most of these questions, you might consider a career as a law enforcement and security officer. To find out more about this job, read on.

Let's Talk Money

Military jobs pay according to seniority, and for the first three years annual salaries do not rise above $20,000. Benefits include tuition support and health and life insurance. The median annual salary for civilian police officers is nearly $50,000, according to 2006 data from the U.S. Bureau of Labor Statistics.

What You'll Do

The work of law enforcement and security specialists is often similar to the work of a civilian police officer. You would control traffic, prevent crime, and respond to emergencies. You'd patrol an assigned area on foot, by car, or by boat to prevent crimes and enforce military rules and regulations. To do this, you may search people, vehicles, property, and places. You may have to pursue suspects, control those who resist apprehension, and even use firearms and other weapons. All of these tasks require you to retain your self-control in potentially explosive situations.

However, you would also have military-specific duties. Law enforcement specialists guard the entrances to military bases and direct the movement of people and traffic. You might have to guard inmates in military correctional facilities. When the United States invaded Iraq in 2003, many law enforcement specialists were used to control the large numbers of detainees being held by U.S. forces. Military police were also assigned to conduct raids and participate in regular patrols.

Another military-specific duty would be to investigate criminal activities and activities related to espionage, treason, and terrorism. This might involve interviewing witnesses, victims, suspects, collecting fingerprints and other evidence, and arresting criminal suspects. You might have to testify or present evidence in a military court proceeding.

In the coast guard or the navy, you also have the responsibility to protect important ports—both overseas and in the United States—against the threat of terrorism and other acts of maritime crime.

Who You'll Work For

✯ All five branches. The army, navy, air force, Marine Corps, and coast guard all need service members who maintain discipline and enforce the law.

✴ A variety of subdivisions. The Military Police Corps serves as the law enforcement arm of the U.S. Army, while the Marine Corps version is known as the Provost Marshal's Office. In the navy, law enforcement personnel are assigned to the Master-at-Arms branch. The Air Force Security Forces police the U.S. Air Force.

Where You'll Work

Law enforcement and security specialists in the military might work indoors or outdoors depending on their assignment. Some have desk jobs and work in air-conditioned comfort. Others conduct investigations or patrol facilities and are at the mercy of the weather. Law enforcement and security specialists, like police officers, face dangerous and unpredictable situations. They must go anywhere a crime is committed, regardless of location, time of day, and climate.

The navy's law force is deployed to many spots worldwide, including Iraq, Afghanistan, and in southern Africa. They may be assigned to a mobile security force detachment, performing missions that involve boarding ships with minimal defense capability, fortifying landside locations, and securing foreign ports for use by U.S. warships.

In civilian life, positions such as a police officer can be found throughout the United States. In 2007, police officers held more than 700,000 jobs.

Your Typical Day

Here are some highlights for a typical day as a law enforcement and security specialist in a combat zone.

✓ **Clear a supply route.** You might be ordered to monitor a major supply route in Iraq. You'll be briefed at 6:30 a.m. and then drive the route to the checkpoint. You'll look for hostile activity, enemy personnel, or anything that looks out of place from previous runs.

Let's Talk Trends

Fear of terrorism has increased the demand for military police services. For example, the number of navy law enforcement specialists has expanded from about 3,500 to 10,000. This is due to their expanding role in antiterrorism protection duties, rather than in law enforcement.

✓ **Report trouble.** Once you travel the route and are sure it is clear, you'll radio back to the convoy commanders and let them know it's safe. If you find something suspicious, you will radio back to headquarters and traffic on the route will be stopped.

✓ **Look for trouble.** After the convoy is clear, you might stop along the route and wait for trouble. This might include improvised explosive devices (IEDs), small arms fire, or vehicle breakdowns.

What You Can Do Now

✴ Work at the mall. Even a part-time security job at the mall will give you a feel for this kind of work. It will also look good when it comes time to choose a career specialty in the military.

✴ Take some college-level classes. People with some training in police science, criminal justice, or law enforcement have a huge edge in receiving their career choice. Any prior experience in law enforcement or military experience with combat skills is extremely valuable.

✴ Join student trooper programs. Many high schools or local forces offer training programs for high school students.

✴ Make sure you are physically fit. Many law enforcement positions require strength, stamina, and agility.

What Training You'll Need

Job training for a law enforcement and security specialists in the armed forces usually consists of about nine weeks of basic training followed by 8 to 12 weeks of individual training and on-the-job instruction. Training length varies depending on specialty.

Law enforcement training includes instruction in military rules and regulations. You will also receive training in the use of firearms, self-defense, first aid, and emergency response. Instructors also teach prisoner control and discipline, investigation and evidence collection procedures, communication skills, traffic and crowd control techniques, and the use of different types of law enforcement equipment. Your training will also probably include on-the-job experience with a veteran officer.

Some branches have training that is more specific. For the U.S. Air Force, security forces students attend the Air Force Security Forces Academy at Lackland Air Force Base in Texas. They must

The Inside Scoop: Q&A

Charles Marren
Provost sergeant
Marine Corps Headquarters, Washington, D.C.

Q: *How did you get your job?*

A: After completing one year of study in criminal justice at Northeastern University in Boston, I began looking for a different kind of challenge. I felt as though I was doing many of the same things I had done in high school. Seeking a way to prove myself, I enlisted in the Marine Corps as a military police officer (MP) at Camp Pendleton, where I performed base security duties.

Q: *What do you like best about your job?*

A: I like the training and travel. I had the opportunity to attend the Federal Bureau of Investigation (FBI) National Academy . . . This enabled me to advance further in the criminal investigation arena. As an investigator, I gathered crime evidence, interrogated suspects, and interviewed witnesses . . . I also had the opportunity to travel to Hawaii, Japan, and other locations.

Q: *What's the most challenging part of your job?*

A: The role of a patrol officer enforcing laws within the base community [has been most challenging for me]. In this position, I responded to emergency situations such as robberies, assaults, and accidents.

Q: *What are the keys to success for your job?*

A: [One key was receiving] extensive investigative training . . . at the FBI National Academy.

complete a 65-day course that teaches basic military police functions, including missile security, convoy actions, capture and recovery of nuclear weapons, law enforcement and directing traffic. The course also teaches nonlethal tactics, such as using pepper spray and pressure points on a body to subdue people.

In the military, you may be able to receive specialized training in a single type of security work such as chemical analysis, firearms instruction, or handwriting and fingerprint identification. For example, at the U.S. Army Military Police School, you can take courses in areas such as crisis/hostage negotiations, military working-dog handling, and weapons of mass destruction crime scene processing.

How to Talk Like a Pro

Here are a few words you'll hear in this career:

* ✯ **AWOL** U.S. military personnel become AWOL (absent without official leave) when they are absent from their post without a valid pass or leave. The Marine Corps and navy usually refer to this as UA, or "unauthorized absence." Law enforcement personnel have to find these people, often known as deserters.
* ✯ **Master-at-Arms** In the U.S. Navy, Master-at-Arms is the specialty concerned with law enforcement and police work.
* ✯ **MP** This is the acronym for "military police," the law enforcement branch of the U.S. Army.
* ✯ **MSST** MSSTs (maritime safety and security teams) are organized by the U.S. Coast Guard. They can be deployed anywhere in the country to provide increased security on the water or the shore.
* ✯ **10-24** Military police code for a suspicious person.

How to Find a Job

Many young men and women enlist in the armed forces right out of high school. An 18-year old high school graduate can walk into the local recruiter's office and enlist. Seventeen-year-olds can also enlist but need a parent's permission.

To serve in the U.S. military, a person must pass physical requirements and a background check. For the army, service obligations are determined at the recruiter's office. You can agree with the recruiter to serve for two, three, four, or even five years. In the Marine Corps, the initial time commitment is usually four to six years. (Read the fine print of your service contract carefully before you agree to sign anything to understand your potential length of service and number of tours of duty.)

In civilian life, most police departments require at least a high school diploma. Police positions are also controlled by civil service regulations, so you will have to take a written examination and then be interviewed by senior officers. You will also take a physical exam, which typically include tests of vision, hearing, strength, and agility. You can get additional information about becoming a police officer from local, state, and federal law enforcement agencies.

Secrets for Success

See the following suggestions and turn to the appendix for advice on résumés and interviews.

★ Develop good judgment. Military police work requires good judgment and faultless ethical behavior in all situations.

★ Have quick reactions. One of the keys to the job is to maintain alertness in extreme conditions, particularly when preceded by long periods of boredom or relatively low stress.

Reality Check

Police work, whether military or civilian, can be stressful and dangerous. Police officers always need to be ready to deal with threatening situations. Law enforcement officers often witness the death and suffering that result from accidents and crimes. A career in law enforcement can put some individuals at risk of depression.

Some Other Jobs to Think About

★ Correctional officer. A correctional officer guards and supervises inmates in a prison or jail. It's a law enforcement job with more routine work.

★ Security guard. Security guards are sometimes confused with the police because of similar uniforms and responsibilities. However, a security guard's power comes from a private contract, not from the government.

★ Private detective or investigator. These jobs are similar to police work. They involve collecting evidence and conducting investigations and surveillance.

How You Can Move Up

✯ Advance in the military. In the armed forces, promotions are awarded based on time in service and merit. After four years, you can achieve a supervisory job such as a squad leader. After 18 years, you can rise to the level of law enforcement superintendent. These officers manage security forces on larger bases.

✯ Advance in civilian life. Civilian law enforcement and security specialists work for state, county, or city law enforcement agencies. They may also work in prisons, intelligence agencies, and private security companies. In most civilian police departments, promotions to detective, corporal, and higher positions are usually based on a combination of your score on a written examination and your on-the-job performance.

Web Sites to Surf

Careers in the Military. This Web site is the starting point for any investigation of jobs in the armed forces. It includes many useful job descriptions and links. http://www.careersinthemilitary.com

Today's Military. This site gives in-depth information on each branch of the U.S. armed forces. http://www.todaysmilitary.com

U.S. Army Military Police School. This is the official site and contains specific information as well as useful links. http://www.wood.army.mil/usamps

Prepare and cook meals

Food Service Specialist/ Cook

Practice the culinary arts

Boost military morale

Food Service Specialist/Cook

It is easy to forget, but food preparation is a crucial military job. After all, soldiers and sailors have to eat. As Napoleon Bonaparte famously said, "an army travels on its stomach." Every day, the U.S. military serves more than one million meals. Some kitchens serve thousands of meals at a time. Others prepare food for small groups of people. Food service specialists operate kitchen and dining facilities. They prepare all types of food. They also order and inspect food supplies. If you enjoy the culinary arts and possess excellent organizational and people skills, then a food service specialist might be the career field for you.

Is This Job for You?

Would working as a food service specialist be a good fit for you? To find out, read each of the following questions and answer "Yes" or "No."

Yes	*No*	**1.**	Are you interested in cooking and food preparation?
Yes	*No*	**2.**	Do you have high standards of personal cleanliness?
Yes	*No*	**3.**	Do you have an interest in nutrition and health?
Yes	*No*	**4.**	Can you understand and follow basic instructions easily?
Yes	*No*	**5.**	Do you like to work with your hands?
Yes	*No*	**6.**	Does the idea of feeding others give you pleasure?
Yes	*No*	**7.**	Are you good at math (for recipe conversions)?
Yes	*No*	**8.**	Can you work well as part of a team?
Yes	*No*	**9.**	Can you work efficiently under pressure?
Yes	*No*	**10.**	Can you stand on your feet all day if necessary?

If you answered "Yes" to most of these questions, you might consider a career as a food service specialist. To find out more about this job, read on.

What You'll Do

As a food service specialist, you would be responsible for the preparation and service of food on the battlefield or back at the base. This means that you would need to estimate food requirements, and then

Let's Talk Money

The federal government pay scale starts low and ends low but includes excellent benefits. Base salary is $20,000 or less for the first three years of service. Military benefits include career training, health care, and money for college. In civilian life, the wages of cooks vary greatly. According to the U.S. Bureau of Labor Statistics, the mean annual salary for chefs and head cooks in 2006 was $38,880, while institutional, cafeteria, and restaurant cooks averaged about $21,000 per year.

order, receive, inspect, and store meat, fish, fruit, and vegetables. Menus would have to be prepared, budgets arranged and followed, and records carefully kept.

Your most important duty would be to feed service members. You'd measure, mix, prepare, and cook ingredients according to recipes. Of course, this would require the knowledge of equipment such as ovens, broilers, grills, slicers, and blenders, and an understanding of the use of a variety of cutlery and pots and pans. During all food prep, you would make sure to follow proper procedures, cooking times, and temperatures. When the food is finally prepared and served, you would supervise or carry out general housekeeping duties; after all, the mess in the kitchen has to be cleaned up when the meal is over.

In the old days, military meals consisted of one or two entrées with vegetables. For breakfast, the only choices were scrambled eggs, cereal, bacon, and toast. There were few healthy choices and no junk food. Those days are long gone. Today, most dining facilities give the choice of a full meal with multiple entrées, including burgers, hot dogs, sandwiches, fries, and chicken. For individuals concerned with health and nutrition, there is usually a "healthy-heart" menu and a salad bar. For breakfast, a service member can choose anything from a small fruit cup to a huge made-to-order omelet with side dishes.

Of course, if a service member is in combat, he or she does not have time for a sit-down meal. In this case, he or she eats an individual MRE (meal, ready-to-eat), a self-contained meal that provides all the nutrition a service member on a mission needs.

Whether you are on a submarine, an air base, or in a combat zone, your skills in preparing food would not only feed people but also help to maintain the morale of your fellow service members.

Let's Talk Trends

The number of food service specialists depends on the size of the military. This can vary widely from year to year. When the U.S. military is fighting a war overseas, the need for food service specialists obviously increases, but private contracting offsets the number of food specialist positions. However, even with outsourcing, there should always be opportunities for military cooks. In civilian life, job openings for chefs, cooks, and food preparation workers are expected to be plentiful through 2017.

Who You'll Work For

✯ All five branches. Obviously, everyone in the U.S. armed forces has to eat. The army, navy, air force, Marine Corps, and coast guard all need food service specialists.

✯ Contract operations. The U.S. armed forces now contracts out many dining facilities to private, nonmilitary companies. At large installations, the cooks are usually civilians employed by contractors. There are still openings for military "cooks," but there is a definite trend to outsourcing.

Where You'll Work

Food service specialists work in just about every duty station available throughout the United States and various locations overseas. Food service specialists can be found in a number of different settings. You may be responsible for cooking or supervising kitchen workers in dining halls, hospitals, field kitchens, or aboard a ship. You might work in refrigerated meat lockers. Occasionally, you'd work outdoors in tents while preparing and serving food under field conditions. A navy cook might cook on a ship's deck for a barbecue known as a "steel beach picnic." Other military cooks prepare meals for dignitaries and other distinguished guests when visiting other countries.

Military food service specialists usually work in clean, well-ventilated, and decently lit kitchens and dining facilities. Most military kitchens have modern equipment, convenient work areas, and some even have air-conditioning. Obviously, conditions in the field or

The Inside Scoop: Q&A

Dwane Robinson
Food services supervisor
USS *Wadsworth*

Q: *How did you get your job?*

A: I joined the navy right after high school to travel and to learn a trade. After spending part of my first tour as a seaman apprentice working in the mess hall, I discovered that cooking was what I wanted to do. My first assignment was on the USS *Waldron* in Norfolk, Virginia, where I worked in the ship's galley.

Q: *What do you like best about your job?*

A: I have spent the past several years as a food services supervisor on different ships and have done what I wanted to do—learn to cook and travel around the world.

Q: *What's the most challenging part of your job?*

A: [As a] senior chef on the USS *New Orleans*, I managed a 35-person staff that fed 580 crew members and, at times, 1,800 marines (nearly 7,000 meals a day).

Q: *What are the keys to success to being a food service specialist?*

A: Through the navy, I went to cooking school to learn more about menu planning, nutrition, and cooking skills. After cooking school, my career really took off . . . I was assigned to the USS *O'Callahan* to be in charge of running the entire mess. At that time, I was also promoted to chief petty officer. The most important day of my career was the day that I put on the hat, signifying that I had become a chef.

in combat zones are less than ideal and working conditions can vary dramatically. Food service specialists usually share small spaces with hot stoves and ovens. They are under constant pressure to prepare meals quickly, yet ensure that quality is maintained and safety and sanitation guidelines are observed.

Your Typical Day

Here are some highlights for a typical day as a food service specialist.

✓ **Check inventory and order supplies.** If you're cooking omelets for 350 soldiers, you had better make sure you have enough eggs or some troops will be very unhappy.

✓ **Prepare the meal.** Cooks cook; it's that simple. You may prepare omelets, cook waffles, pancakes, and grits. Other meals may include steaks, chops, and roasts, or you may bake or fry chicken, turkey, and fish. You might also prepare gravies and sauces and bake breads, cakes, pies, and pastries.

✓ **Supervise clean up.** You probably won't have to scrub out the pots, but it's your job to make sure they are all clean and sanitary. Ovens, stoves, mixers, and utensils all have to be spotless. Food poisoning could incapacitate a whole platoon.

What You Can Do Now

✯ Take relevant classes in high school. Helpful school subjects include cooking classes, nutrition and related classes, health, mathematics, accounting, and chemistry.

✯ Take a specialized course. Community colleges and vocational schools offer specialized classes in cooking and food service.

✯ Get some experience. Most fast-food or short-order cooks require little education or training; most skills are learned on the job. The more experience you have, the more it will help you in this field.

What Training You'll Need

Job training for a food service specialist begins with nine weeks of basic training. Even food service specialists must learn basic soldiering skills. This is followed by about 8 to 12 weeks of advanced individual training, including practice in food preparation. The length of your training depends on your particular job specialty. Part of this time will be spent in the classroom and part in on-the-job training in the kitchen.

As a food service specialist, you'll study standard and dietetic menus and recipes and food preparation. You'll also learn related skills such as how to order food and supplies, how to properly use and care for kitchen equipment, and how to store perishable food items. Other subjects include the safe use of equipment, recipe conversions, basic food preparation terminology, and sanitation.

At first, you'll prepare ingredients and cook basic dishes under the supervision of experienced cooks. You'll probably be responsible for maintaining the kitchen in a clean, orderly fashion. Over time, your responsibilities will expand and soon you will be cooking for hundreds.

Food service specialists may branch out into other areas beyond culinary arts. After initial study, you can acquire further training in accounting, administration and management, nutritional cooking, dining facility management, and entertainment services. You might also study computer accounting and inventory software in order to better keep track of the vast quantities of food used by the military. Some of your formal and on-the-job training will transfer to college credit hours. You can use this credit toward an associate's or bachelor's degree.

How to Talk Like a Pro

Here are a few words you'll hear in this career:

* **Cambro** A large plastic pan used for storage. The term comes from the company that makes these containers. They are also referred to as a Lexan, a name taken from a competing company.
* **DFAC** Abbreviation for "dining facilities administration center," in other words, a cafeteria or mess hall.
* **Galley** The area on a ship where meals are prepared.
* **KP** Short for "kitchen patrol." This is a one-day duty assignment for soldiers to do mess hall work. They might help prepare food, clean out grease traps, or most famously, peel potatoes.
* **Mess** A meal.

How to Find a Job

Many young men and women enlist in the armed forces right out of high school. At 18 years old you can sign up on your own; if you're 17, you can do so with a parent's permission.

To serve in the U.S. military, a person must pass physical requirements and a background check. For the army, your service obligations would be determined at the recruiter's office. You can agree with the recruiter to serve for two, three, four, or even five years. (Read the fine print of your service contract carefully before you agree to sign anything to understand your proposed length or service and number of tours of duty.)

In civilian life, cooks' jobs are frequently advertised in newspapers and on the Web. Because turnover is high in entry-level positions, the best source may be word-of-mouth.

Secrets for Success

See the following suggestions and turn to the appendix for advice on résumés and interviews.

* Have a thick skin. No matter how well you cook, it's traditional for service members to complain about the food. You will have to get used to the griping and just deal with it.
* There's no place like the U.S. armed services for a diverse population. You may have the opportunity to learn a lot about cuisines from many cultures—and this could propel you in a career of cooking if you decide to pursue one.

Reality Check

A career as a cook can get stale quickly. You're standing for hours at a time, lifting heavy pots and pans, and working around hot ovens and grills. Be prepared to do a lot of sweating. Also, if you want to cook for service men and women, consider applying directly with a food-service contractor, such as KBR (formerly Kellogg, Brown and Root). You won't need to make as lengthy of a commitment.

Some Other Jobs to Think About

* Cook. If you can get the experience or training out of the military, there are thousands of job possibilities in the civilian world.
* Restaurant owner. If you are an entrepreneur with access to start-up money, you can own your own business.
* Caterer. This food service specialty combines cooking with entrepreneurship. You'll get to serve more interesting food than in the military.

How You Can Move Up

✸ Advance in the military. In the armed forces, promotions can come quickly based on time in service and merit. After seven years, you can become a chef. Chefs plan and prepare food menus and recipes and direct kitchen staff. After 15 years, you can advance as high as food service supervisor. These officers plan budgets, monitor food service expenses, and determine personnel, equipment, and food supply needs.

✸ Advance in civilian life. The skills you learn as a food service specialist will allow you to work in civilian restaurants, cafeterias, hotels, hospitals, manufacturing plants, schools, and other organizations that have their own dining facilities. You can advance by taking classes at a technical school or two-year college to specialize in desserts, advanced cooking techniques, cooking for banquets or parties, and cooking styles from around the world. The American Culinary Federation accredits more than 100 formal training programs and sponsors apprenticeship programs around the country.

Web Sites to Surf

Careers in the Military. This Web site is the starting point for any investigation of jobs in the armed forces. It includes many useful job descriptions and links. http://www.careersinthemilitary.com

Today's Military. This site gives in-depth information on each branch of the U.S. armed forces. http://www.todaysmilitary.com

The American Culinary Federation. The federation has 19,000 members and is the main professional chefs' organization in North America. This Web site has information on apprenticeship and certification programs and a career center. http://www.acfchefs.org

National Restaurant Association. This Web site includes a directory of two- and four-year colleges that offer food service career courses. http://www.restaurant.org

Keep the military mobile

Cargo Specialist

Ensure essential supplies arrive on time

Load and store gear and equipment

Cargo Specialist

Imagine that you're a soldier in a firefight. You reach for another clip of ammunition—but there's none left! Your platoon is short of ammunition, so you are left unarmed. Cargo specialists make sure this sort of scenario does not become a reality. They try to ensure that the proper supplies arrive safely, on time, and at the correct destination. They are responsible for seeing that planes do not leave runways and ships do not leave ports without spare parts, cargo, and other equipment.

The U.S. armed forces is very large and very mobile. The military has to deliver supplies, weapons, food, equipment, and mail to U.S. forces in many locations throughout the world. In addition, thousands of service men and women constantly need to be moved from one place to another. Wherever cargo specialists are stationed, they play a crucial role in allowing the U.S. military to function.

Is This Job for You?

Would working as a cargo specialist be a good fit for you? To find out, read each of the following questions and answer "Yes" or "No."

Yes	*No*	**1.**	Do you like working with machines such as forklifts and cranes?
Yes	*No*	**2.**	Are you organized and detail-oriented?
Yes	*No*	**3.**	Do you like a job that includes some physical work?
Yes	*No*	**4.**	Are you familiar with basic computer programs?
Yes	*No*	**5.**	Do you enjoy troubleshooting problems?
Yes	*No*	**6.**	Are you particularly honest?
Yes	*No*	**7.**	Do you have typing and keyboarding skills?
Yes	*No*	**8.**	Are you interested in logistics and business mathematics?
Yes	*No*	**9.**	Do you enjoy a job that includes some filing and recordkeeping?
Yes	*No*	**10.**	Do you enjoy work that emphasizes accuracy?

If you answered "Yes" to most of these questions, you might consider a career as a cargo specialist. To find out more about this job, read on.

Let's Talk Money

A private with a year of experience earns a base base salary of $16,000, and a corporal with three years' experience makes about $20,000 per year. Military benefits include career training, health care, money for college, and life insurance. In civilian life, cargo and freight agents earn an average of about $38,560 a year, according to 2006 data from the Bureau of Labor Statistics.

What You Will Do

As a cargo specialist, you would see that the materials and equipment that members of the U.S. armed forces need are available and arrive safely at the correct destinations. It would be your job to transfer or supervise the transfer of cargo as it travels by land, water, and air transport. Keeping the military's supply system operating smoothly is an extremely vital job. The lives of troops in the field depend on receiving the right supplies on time.

Cargo specialists may perform two different types of duties. On one hand, their work can require physical strength and hands-on use of machinery. Cargo specialists load and unload supplies and material from airplanes, ships, docks, boxcars, warehouses, and trucks. To do this, they use forklifts and winches. Equipment such as jeeps, trucks, and weapons must be loaded aboard ships using dockyard cranes. Cargo specialists may have to carefully pack and crate boxes of supplies for shipping.

On the other hand, working as a cargo specialist has a white-collar component. You could be responsible for knowing the status and location of your shipments. Cargo specialists plan and organize loading schedules and often track shipments electronically using bar codes. When freight arrives, you would have to check the shipment against the invoice to make sure that there is no damage and that the amount and destination of material are correct. Cargo specialists also have to prepare inventory reports, write correspondence, and keep cost-related records.

Who You'll Work For

✯ Army
✯ Navy

⭐ Air force
⭐ Coast guard

Where You'll Work

The working environment of cargo specialists may vary considerably. Some may work in a one-person office and have the sole responsibility for all fiscal (budgetary) and supply records. Others might work in a team supervising a 60-person warehouse. Cargo specialists also can be found in warehouses, stockrooms, loading docks, cold storage rooms, and shipping and receiving rooms, which may not be temperature controlled.

Machines and computers have reduced the physical demands of working with freight. However, the work still can be strenuous, even though material-handling equipment moves heavier items. Many jobs for cargo specialists still involve frequent standing, bending, walking, and stretching. Lifting and carrying smaller items is also common.

Cargo specialists usually work regular schedules and hours but this depends entirely on where you are stationed. Evening and weekend hours can be common and extra work may be required if a large shipment comes in or needs to go out.

Your Typical Day

Here are some highlights for a typical day as a cargo specialist at Ramstein Air Base in Germany.

Let's Talk Trends

The number of military cargo specialists depends on the mission of the U.S. armed forces in any given year. For example, if the U.S. is fighting a war overseas, such as in Iraq, the number of cargo specialists needed by the military greatly increases. In general, the number of cargo specialists is expected to decrease due to advances in technology and automation. However, buying over the Internet will result in additional shipments and may help to create job openings. In civilian life, cargo and freight agents held about 70,000 jobs in 2007. About one in five of these positions worked in the air transportation industry.

✓ **Check invoices.** Most U.S. military cargo arrives in Europe on boats and travels to Ramstein by truck. You will have to crosscheck this cargo against the invoices to make sure the amounts and destination of materials are correct. You also will have to inspect the cargo for damage.

✓ **Load supplies for Southwest Asia.** Each day, cargo specialists at Ramstein load about 20 aircraft full of cargo. That is about 300 tons of cargo a day arriving at the base and leaving on transit planes. You'll supervise the packing and crating of boxes for shipping and inspect the loads for balance and safety.

✓ **Keep track of cargo.** You will use computers to track and maintain inventory and freight. You will also track the movement of troops. About 1,000 service members a day move through Ramstein on their way to or from Iraq and Afghanistan.

What You Can Do Now

✯ Take useful courses in school. Helpful subjects include general office skills and business math.

✯ Get a part-time warehouse job. During the holidays, warehouses need extra help. This is a great time to pick up valuable experience with cranes and forklifts as well as get a feel for whether you like this type of work.

✯ Make sure your computer skills are up to date. The job of a cargo specialist is becoming increasingly automated. You have to be comfortable working with computers to be successful.

What Training You'll Need

To become a cargo specialist in the armed forces, you will first undergo nine weeks of basic training. This is followed by about eight weeks of individual training including classroom instruction and on-the-job practice in loading cargo.

When you start working, you'll use forklifts, power winches, and cranes to load and unload freight. You'll learn techniques for loading and storing cargo and the planning and scheduling of cargo shipments. Your instructors will also cover proper safety procedures, especially for handling dangerous cargo such as ammunition.

Cargo specialists check items to be shipped, attach labels to them, and then make sure that the addresses are correct. This requires

The Inside Scoop: Q&A

Douglas Kronchek
Deputy chief of staff
Joint Forces Command—Norfolk, Virginia

Q: *How did you get your job?*

A: I enlisted in the army shortly after high school and did so well in aircraft maintenance training, I was encouraged to apply for Officer Candidate School where I earned my commission. I chose the transportation corps because I wanted to stay close to aircraft and maintenance.

Q: *What do you like best about your job?*

A: A high point in my career was a two-year tour as the army port and air terminal expert with the navy. I arranged the transportation to move people and supplies to and from the U.S. scientific research stations in Antarctica. I worked with private and government transportation agencies and officials from the United States, Australia, and New Zealand.

Q: *What's the most challenging part of your job?*

A: I . . . spent several years at the Pentagon in Washington, D.C., as chief logistician for the Pacific (after I earned a master's degree in logistics and transportation). I was the expert on all army transportation and supply activity in the Pacific, and later my command controlled the movement of army personnel, equipment, and supplies to destinations all around the world.

Q: *What are the keys to success to being a cargo specialist?*

A: In the Marine Corps, I have always valued . . . hard work and effort. (Also key is) a sense of camaraderie and commitment.

training in the use of automated equipment. Some of this training is done on the job. However, as the occupation becomes more automated, longer periods of training are required in order to learn the use of the new equipment. Your training in the military will probably be ongoing.

As you are promoted over time, you will get further from the actual dirty work of shipping. Advanced-level cargo specialists supervise and train other service members for cargo handling equipment such as cranes and forklifts. More advanced technical and operational training is also available during your later career. Some of the training you'll receive may be applied as credit hours toward a bachelor's or associate's degree.

How to Talk Like a Pro

Here are a few words you'll hear in this career:

* ✯ **Box stretcher** A U.S. Air Force term for a make-believe device that will stretch a piece of cargo so that it will leave no space on an aircraft pallet.
* ✯ **Five-ton** Any truck that has a cargo capacity of about five tons.
* ✯ **GVW** An abbreviation for "Gross Vehicle Weight." It represents the total weight of a loaded vehicle, including chassis, body, and freight.
* ✯ **Mule** A small four-wheeled cargo vehicle.
* ✯ **Permits** Permission granted to carriers by states to transport freight exceeding legal weight and size limits

How to Find a Job

Many young men and women enlist in the armed forces right out of high school. An 18-year old high school graduate can walk into the local recruiter's office and enlist. Seventeen-year-olds can also enlist but need a parent's permission.

To serve in the U.S. military, a person must pass physical requirements and a background check. For most branches of the armed forces, your service obligations would be determined at the recruiter's office. You can agree with the recruiter to serve for two, three, four, or even five years. (Read the fine print of your service contract carefully before you agree to sign anything to understand your potential length of service and number of tours of duty.)

In civilian life, work in the transportation field can be acquired through the newspaper or Internet. However, community colleges or vocational schools that offer classes in the field usually have better information about job openings.

Secrets for Success

See the following suggestions and turn to the appendix for advice on résumés and interviews.

★ Have a knack for organization. Cargo specialists have to remember types of freight, quantities, and destinations. An ability to mentally categorize, classify, and systematize is an important strength for this field.

★ Don't be afraid of the dark. When you find something you don't know, use it as chance to learn something new. Ask a friendly colleague to fill you in on the workings of a process or machine you need to understand.

Reality Check

Cargo specialists have to be master problem solvers, as equipment and supplies face delays, packing errors, and other holdups. This means cargo specialists are often in the crosshairs of those anxious to receive essential supplies.

Some Other Jobs to Think About

★ Truck driver. Why not travel with your cargo? Truck drivers deliver everything from automobiles to canned food.

★ Forklift operator. Forklifts move heavy objects around warehouses, storage yards, factories, or construction sites. The job has some prestige in a warehouse.

★ Bookkeeper. Bookkeepers are an organization's financial record keepers. They make numerous computations each day and use computers to calculate and record data.

How You Can Move Up

★ Advance in the military. In the armed forces, promotions are based on time in service and merit. Career paths for cargo specialists include moving up to supply and warehousing manager or transportation manager. These are supervisory positions with more budgetary and planning responsibilities.

✯ Advance in civilian life. In civilian life, cargo specialists work for trucking firms, air cargo companies, and shipping lines. Jobs in these fields include industrial truck operators, dockworkers, and cargo and freight agents. You can usually advance to a shipping manager's position simply based on experience and knowledge of warehouse computer systems such as EDI (electronic data interchange). Skills can be learned at almost any technical or two-year college.

Web Sites to Surf

Careers in the Military. This Web site is the starting point for any investigation of jobs in the armed forces. It includes many useful job descriptions and links. http://www.careersinthemilitary.com

Today's Military. This site gives in-depth information on each branch of the U.S. armed forces. http://www.todaysmilitary.com

International Air Cargo Association. The association is a lobbying organization, but their site offers basic information about the industry. http://www.tiaca.org

International Air Cargo Association of Chicago. This Web site contains good links and some educational/scholarship information. http://www.iacac.com

Keep planes safely airborne

Aircraft Mechanic

Solve complex mechanical problems

Work with cutting-edge equipment

Aircraft Mechanic

Does the idea of working with some of the world's most high-tech aircraft and equipment sound cool? As a military aircraft mechanic, you would tinker with the newest electronics and repair aircraft so that they remain safe and ready to fly. The U.S. military uses a wide range of helicopters and airplanes to move people and equipment during military operations. Countless military missions depend on aircraft for patrol, transport, and flight training. Not a single helicopter, jet fighter, or cargo plane leaves the runway or the flight deck without the support of well-trained aircraft mechanics.

Is This Job for You?

Would working as an aircraft mechanic be a good fit for you? To find out, read each of the following questions and answer "Yes" or "No."

Yes	No	**1.**	Do you like using your hands and power tools?
Yes	No	**2.**	Do you have an interest in working with aircraft?
Yes	No	**3.**	Could you deal with the pressure of making life-and-death repairs?
Yes	No	**4.**	Do you possess good communication skills?
Yes	No	**5.**	Do you have a good memory?
Yes	No	**6.**	Are you interested in engine mechanics?
Yes	No	**7.**	Do you have excellent problem-solving skills?
Yes	No	**8.**	Can you understand and process new information?
Yes	No	**9.**	Do you like taking classes in mathematics and shop mechanics?
Yes	No	**10.**	Do you quickly comprehend what you have read?

If you answered "Yes" to most of these questions, you might consider a career as an aircraft mechanic. To find out more about this job, read on.

What You'll Do

Military aircraft mechanics inspect, service, and repair helicopters and airplanes. However, as an aircraft mechanic, you will have a range of career subspecialties. Aircraft are very complex machines

Let's Talk Money

Privates and corporals, with one and three years' experience, respectively, draw base annual salaries of $16,000 and $20,000, respectively. Benefits packages for military personnel are excellent and include career training, health care, tuition support, and life insurance. Most soldiers on active duty also receive a housing allowance, a subsistence allowance, combat pay, and other benefits. In civilian life, the average annual salary for aircraft mechanics is about $49,300, according to 2006 data from the U.S. the Bureau of Labor Statistics.

composed of many different systems that need frequent servicing. You might work on specific types of aircraft, such as jets, propeller planes, or helicopters. Or you might specialize in one section of a particular type of aircraft, such as the engine or electrical system.

Airframe mechanics work on any part of the aircraft except the instruments, powerplants, and propellers. Powerplant mechanics work on engines and perform some work on propellers. Airframe-and-powerplant mechanics (A&P mechanics) work on all parts of the plane except the instruments. The majority of mechanics working on civilian aircraft are A&P mechanics. In the military, however, most aircraft mechanics specialize on very particular types of planes.

Some aircraft mechanics concentrate on repairing electrical systems. Instruments, lights, weapons, ignition systems, and landing gear all use electricity. If something is defective, such as a generator or wiring, mechanics repair or replace it. The increasing use of technology has led to more mechanics working on repairing electronic systems, such as computerized controls and radar systems. However, structural mechanics repair and replace nonelectric parts such as longerons, bulkheads, beams, and aircraft skin.

Many aircraft mechanics specialize in preventive maintenance. They inspect engines, brakes, valves, pumps, and air-conditioning systems to make sure they are in good working order. These mechanics repair and replace worn or defective parts and keep records related to the maintenance. For example, a typical C-5 cargo plane requires about 20 hours of maintenance for every hour of flying time.

Whether specializing in electronics, hydraulics, engines, maintenance, or any other field, aircraft mechanics must test the equipment

Let's Talk Trends

The U.S. military depends on airpower, so there are always opportunities for aircraft mechanics. Civilian airports, airline companies, aircraft manufacturers, and government and law enforcement agencies also need aircraft mechanics. The Bureau of Labor Statistics estimates that jobs for aircraft mechanics should increase about as fast as average through the year 2014.

to make sure that it works properly after they repair it. They work as quickly as safety permits so that the aircraft can return to service without delay. In this way, an aircraft mechanic's skills are vital to the successful operation of the U.S. military.

Who You'll Work For

* Army
* Navy
* Air force
* Marine Corps
* Coast guard

Where You'll Work

Most military aircraft mechanics may be stationed anywhere around the world. You may work on a base in the United States, on the flight deck of aircraft carrier off the coast of Lebanon, or on an island in the Pacific.

Aircraft mechanics work in aircraft hangars and machine shops located on air bases or aboard aircraft carriers. Although mechanics usually work indoors, they sometimes work outdoors when hangars are full or when repairs must be made quickly.

Being an aircraft mechanic is a stressful job. Mechanics often work under time pressure to maintain flight schedules; long hours are a frequent problem. This is more of a problem in combat situations. They also have a tremendous responsibility to maintain safety standards. Millions of dollars of equipment, and more importantly, people's lives, depend on their skill and careful work.

The Inside Scoop: Q&A

Brian Goelf
Assistant manager, F-15 maintenance unit
U.S. Pacific Command, Camp H.M. Smith, Hawaii

Q: *How did you get your job?*

A: After basic training, I went to aircraft mechanic's school and field training. After two years of performing unscheduled maintenance (pilot-reported problems) [at Andrews Airforce Base], I went to Goose Bay, Canada, for another field training course on the F-102 aircraft.

Q: *What do you like best about your job?*

A: I saw the air force as a chance to get ahead and establish a good career, but it was having a job I really liked and being able to fly as well that really sold me.

Q: *What's the most challenging part of your job?*

A: [It was serving] as the Pacific Air Force Command manager for several types of aircraft, ensuring that materials and supplies reached air force units in the Pacific. I . . . also [helped manage] a maintenance unit capable of supporting F-15 fighters anywhere in the world.

Q: *What are the keys to success to your job?*

A: [You need to be very] mechanically inclined.

The job has some physical drawbacks. Aircraft mechanics often examine engines by working through specially designed openings while standing on ladders or scaffolds or by using hoists or lifts to remove the entire engine from the craft. Mechanics must lift or pull heavy objects. They often stand, lie, or kneel in awkward positions. Noise and vibration are a constant problem when testing engines. However, wherever you work, you will never question the importance of your job. Every aircraft you take care of has to perform its mission successfully and return home safely.

Your Typical Day

Here are some highlights for a typical day as an aircraft mechanic, who is specializing in electrical repair.

✔ **Perform preflight inspections.** You are responsible for maintaining a squadron of wide-bodied C-5 cargo planes, performing daily pre-flight, and postflight aircraft inspections.

✔ **Rely on inspection equipment.** A pilot reports that his left engine doesn't sound right. You use your skills to help take apart the engine and repair or replace parts. To do this you use precision instruments. You're measuring parts for wear and using X-ray and magnetic inspection equipment to check for invisible cracks.

✔ **Troubleshoot.** During a preflight check, a pilot discovers that her aircraft's fuel gauge doesn't work. To solve the problem, you'll have to troubleshoot the electrical system. You use electrical test equipment to make sure that no wires are broken or shorted out. You discover the defective component and replace it.

What You Can Do Now

✶ Take relevant classes in high school. Courses in math, physics, chemistry, electronics, computer science, and mechanical draw-ing are helpful because they incorporate many of the principles involved in the operation of aircraft. Knowledge of these princi-ples is often necessary to make repairs.

✶ Take a course at a community college or vocational school. It never hurts to have as much specific training as possible.

✶ Learn to fly a plane. You can take classes at your local airfield. It is obviously much easier to understand the field if you have your pilot's license.

What Training You'll Need

Job training for an aircraft mechanic in the armed forces usually consists of about two months of basic training followed by anywhere from 14 to 52 weeks of advanced training. There are numerous sub-specialties within aircraft repair and maintenance. Your length of training depends on which subspecialty you choose or are assigned.

The training you will receive will be a mixture of hands-on experi-ence and classroom study. Some of the skills you might learn include engine disassembly and repair; the inspection and repair of hydraulic, fuel, and electrical systems; and the repair of aluminum, steel, and fiberglass airframes and coverings.

Apprentice military aircraft mechanics work under close supervision and perform routine repair and maintenance duties. They also keep maintenance logs in which any service or repairs are recorded. As new and more complex aircraft are designed, mechanics need ongoing training to update their skills. Most of the training you will receive can be counted toward credit hours for a vocational certificate, as well as towards a college degree.

In civilian life, most aircraft mechanics learn their job in one of about 170 trade schools certified by the Federal Aviation Administration (FAA). About one-third of these schools award two-year and four-year degrees in avionics or aviation technology. FAA training standards are established by law. They require that certified mechanic schools offer students a minimum of 1,900 actual class hours. Coursework in schools normally lasts from 18 to 24 months.

Some aircraft mechanics in the armed forces acquire enough general experience to satisfy the work experience requirements for an FAA certificate. With additional study, they may pass the certifying exam. In general, however, jobs in the military services are too specialized to provide the broad experience required by the FAA. Most armed forces mechanics have to complete the entire training program, although it is possible to receive some credit for the material they learned in the service.

How to Talk Like a Pro

Here are a few words you'll hear in this career:

✴ **Drag** A force such as air resistance that slows an object in motion through the air.
✴ **FOD** An abbreviation for "foreign object damage." Jet engines can suffer major damage when an engine sucks up a rock on the runway or a bird in flight. FOD also includes hail, ice, dust, tools, bolts, and metal shavings. FOD causes damage worth an estimated $4 billion every year.
✴ **Hangar queen** An aircraft with a bad maintenance record that spends a great deal of time being repaired or maintained. Hangar queens are often pirated for spare parts for other aircraft.

✦ **Longeron** In aircraft construction, a longeron is a thin strip of wood or metal, to which the skin of the aircraft is fastened. Longerons are attached to frames (known as formers) in the case of the fuselage, or ribs in the case of a wing.

How to Find a Job

Many young men and women enlist in the armed forces right out of high school. An 18-year old high school graduate can walk into the local recruiter's office and enlist. Seventeen-year-olds can also enlist but need a parent's permission.

To serve in the U.S. military, a person must pass physical requirements and a background check. Academically, an applicant must score at least a 31 on the Armed Forces Qualification Test (AFQT). For the army, your service obligations would be determined at the recruiter's office. You can agree with the recruiter to serve for two, three, four, or even five years. (Read the fine print of your service contract carefully before you agree to sign anything to understand your potential length of service or number of tours of duty.)

For a civilian aircraft mechanic job, military experience is a great advantage when seeking employment. Employers consider applicants with formal training to be the most desirable. In addition, many people in the civilian aviation field have a military background. Jobs are advertised on the Web and with training programs.

Secrets for Success

See the following suggestions and turn to the appendix for advice on résumés and interviews.

✦ Small errors can be fatal. Aircraft mechanics need an almost obsessive concern with details. A leftover pile of metal shavings in an engine can disable a $200 million dollar plane.

✦ Though machines are your focus, people are the most important part of your job. Share information, develop contacts for the future, and learn different styles of getting things one.

Reality Check

If you are hoping to convert directly to a civilian career, you may be disappointed. Few aircraft mechanics in the armed forces acquire enough general experience to satisfy the requirements for an FAA certificate.

Some *Other Jobs to Think About*

✦ Engineer. Workers in engineering use their analytical skills to solve practical problems. In this occupation, you are not restricted to aircraft.

✦ Machinist. In this position, you can make, repair, and modify metal and nonmetal parts for engines and other types of machines.

✦ Carpenters, electricians, plumbers. These are all construction positions that involve problem-solving repairs.

How *You Can Move Up*

✦ Advance in the military. In the armed forces, promotions can come quickly based on time in service and merit. Advanced level aircraft mechanics supervise and train other service members. After 19 years, you can advance as high as Aircraft Maintenance Supervisor. These officers are in charge of large aircraft maintenance and repair facilities. They also plan and direct inspection, service, and modification of aircraft.

✦ Advance in civilian life. The skills you learn as a military aircraft mechanic will help prepare you to work for aircraft manufacturers, commercial airlines and government agencies. Opportunities are plentiful for this type of work but you may have to complete a formal training program. Classes and programs at FAA-certified trade schools will give you the necessary credentials to advance in avionics, aviation technology, or aviation maintenance management.

Web Sites to Surf

Careers in the Military. This Web site is the starting point for any investigation of jobs in the armed forces. It includes many useful job descriptions and links. http://www.careersinthemilitary.com

Today's Military. This site gives in-depth information on each branch of the U.S. armed forces. http://www.todaysmilitary.com

Federal Aviation Administration: Mechanics. This Web site contains more than 20 links to information about licenses, regulations, training, policies, technical information, and forms. http://www.faa.gov/mechanics

Unlock your network

Appendix

Get your résumé ready

Ace your interview

Putting Your Best Foot Forward

When 20-year-old Justin Schulman started job-hunting for a position as a fitness trainer—the first step toward managing a fitness facility—he didn't mess around. "I immediately opened the Yellow Pages and started calling every number listed under health and fitness, inquiring about available positions," he recalls. Schulman's energy and enterprise paid off: He wound up with interviews that led to several offers of part-time work.

Schulman's experience highlights an essential lesson for job seekers: There are plenty of opportunities out there, but jobs won't come to you—especially the career-oriented, well-paying ones that that you'll want to stick with over time. You've got to seek them out.

Uncover Your Interests

Whether you're in high school or bringing home a full-time paycheck, the first step toward landing your ideal job is assessing your interests. You need to figure out what makes you tick. After all, there is a far greater chance that you'll enjoy and succeed in a career that taps into your passions, inclinations, and natural abilities. That's what happened with career-changer Scott Rolfe. He was already 26 when he realized he no longer wanted to work in the food industry. "I'm an avid outdoorsman," Rolfe says, "and I have an appreciation for natural resources that many people take for granted." Rolfe turned his passions into his ideal job as a forestry technician.

If you have a general idea of what your interests are, you're far ahead of the game. You may know that you're cut out for a health care career, for instance, or one in business. You can use a specific volume of Great Careers with a High School Diploma to discover what position to target. If you are unsure of your direction, check out the whole range of volumes to see the scope of jobs available.

You can also use interest inventories and skills-assessment programs to further pinpoint your ideal career. Your school or public librarian or guidance counselor should be able to help you locate such assessments. Web sites, such as America's Career InfoNet (http ://www.acinet.org) and Jobweb.com, also offer interest inventories.

You'll find suggestions for Web sites related to specific careers at the end of each chapter in any Great Careers with a High School Diploma volume.

Unlock Your Network

The next stop toward landing the perfect job is networking. The word may make you cringe, but networking is simply introducing yourself and exchanging job-related and other information that may prove helpful to one or both of you. That's what Susan Tinker-Muller did. Quite a few years ago, she struck up a conversation with a fellow passenger on her commuter train. Little did she know that the natural interest she expressed in the woman's accounts payable department would lead to news about a job opening there. Tinker-Muller's networking landed her an entry-level position in accounts payable with MTV Networks. She is now the accounts payable administrator.

Tinker-Muller's experience illustrates why networking is so important. Fully 80 percent of openings are *never* advertised, and more than half of all employees land their jobs through networking, according to the U.S. Bureau of Labor Statistics. That's 8 out of 10 jobs that you'll miss if you don't get out there and talk with people. And don't think you can bypass face-to-face conversations by posting your résumé on job sites like Craigslist, Monster.com, and Hotjobs.com and then waiting for employers to contact you. That's so mid-1990s! Back then, tens of thousands, if not millions, of job seekers diligently posted their résumés on scores of sites. Then they sat back and waited . . . and waited . . . and waited. You get the idea. Big job sites have their place, of course, but relying solely on an Internet job search is about as effective throwing your résumé into a black hole.

Begin your networking efforts by making a list of people to talk to: teachers, classmates (and their parents), anyone you've worked with, neighbors, members of your church, synogogue, temple or mosque, and anyone you've interned or volunteered with. You can also expand your networking opportunities through the student sections of industry associations; attending or volunteering at industry events, association conferences, career fairs; and through job-shadowing. Keep in mind that only rarely will any of the people on your list be in a position to offer you a job. But whether they know it or not, they probably know someone who knows someone who is. That's why your networking goal is not to ask for a job but the name of someone to talk with. Even when you network with an employer, it's wise to say something like, "You may not have any positions available, but would you know someone I could talk with to find out more about what it's like to work in this field?"

Also, keep in mind that networking is a two-way street. For instance, you may be talking with someone who has a job opening that isn't appropriate for you. If you can refer someone else to the employer, either person may well be disposed to help you someday in the future.

Dial-Up Help

Call your contacts directly, rather than e-mail them. (E-mails are too easy for busy people to ignore, even if they don't mean to.) Explain that you're a recent graduate; that Mr. Jones referred you; and that you're wondering if you could stop by for 10 or 15 minutes at your contact's convenience to find out a little more about how the industry works. If you leave this message as a voicemail, note that you'll call back in a few days to follow up. If you reach your contact directly, expect that they'll say they're too busy at the moment to see you. Ask, "Would you mind if I check back in a couple of weeks?" Then jot down a note in your date book or set up a reminder in your computer calendar and call back when it's time. (Repeat this above scenario as needed, until you get a meeting.)

Once you have arranged to talk with someone in person, prep yourself. Scour industry publications for insightful articles; having up-to-date knowledge about industry trends shows your networking contacts that you're dedicated and focused. Then pull together questions about specific employers and suggestions that will set you apart from the job-hunting pack in your field. The more specific your questions (for instance, about one type of certification versus another), the more likely your contact will see you as an "insider," worthy of passing along to a potential employer. At the end of any networking meeting, ask for the name of someone else who might be able to help you further target your search.

Get a Lift

When you meet with a contact in person (as well as when you run into someone fleetingly), you need an "elevator speech." This is a summary of up to two minutes that introduces who you are, as well as your experience and goals. An elevator speech should be short enough to be delivered during an elevator ride with a potential employer from the ground level to a high floor. In it, it's helpful to show that 1) you know the business involved; 2) you know the company; 3) you're qualified (give your work and educational information); and 4) you're goal-oriented, dependable, and hardworking. You'll be surprised how much information you can include in two minutes. Practice this speech in front of a mirror until you have the key points down very well. It should sound natural though, and you should come across as friendly, confident, and assertive. Remember, good eye contact needs to be part of your presentation as well as your everyday approach when meeting prospective employers or leads.

Get Your Résumé Ready

In addition to your elevator speech, another essential job-hunting tool is your résumé. Basically, a résumé is a little snapshot of you in words, reduced to one 8½ x 11-inch sheet of paper (or, at most, two sheets). You need a résumé whether you're in high school, college, or the workforce, and whether you've never held a job or have had many.

At the top of your résumé should be your heading. This is your name, address, phone numbers, and your e-mail address, which can be a sticking point. E-mail addresses such as sillygirl@yahoo.com or drinkingbuddy@hotmail.com won't score you any points. In fact they're a turn-off. So if you dreamed up your address after a night on the town, maybe it's time to upgrade. (And while we're on the subject, these days, potential employers often check Myspace pages, personal blogs, and Web sites. What's posted there has been known to cost candidates job offers.)

The first section of your résumé is a concise Job Objective: "Entry-level agribusiness sales representative seeking a position with a leading dairy cooperative." These days, with word-processing software, it's easy and smart to adapt your job objective to the position for which you're applying. An alternative way to start a résumé, which some recruiters prefer, is to rework the Job Objective into a Professional Summary. A Professional Summary doesn't mention the position you're seeking, but instead focuses on your job strengths: e.g., "Entry-level agribusiness sales rep; strengths include background in feed, fertilizer, and related markets and ability to contribute as a member of a sales team." Which is better? It's your call.

The body of a résumé typically starts with your Job Experience. This is a chronological list of the positions you've held (particularly the ones that will help you land the job you want). Remember: Never, never fudge anything. It is okay, however, to include volunteer positions and internships on the chronological list, as long as they're noted for what they are.

Next comes your Education section. Note: It's acceptable to flip the order of your Education and Job Experience sections if you're still in high school or don't have significant work experience. Summarize any courses you've taken in the job area you're targeting, any certifications you've achieved, relevant computer knowledge, special seminars, or other school-related experience that will distinguish you. Include your grade average if it's more than 3.0. Don't worry if you haven't finished your degree. Simply write that you're currently enrolled in your program (if you are).

In addition to these elements, other sections may include professional organizations you belong to and any work-related achievements, awards, or recognition you've received. Also, you can have a section for your interests, such as playing piano or soccer (and include any notable achievements regarding your interests, for instance, placed third in Midwest Regional Piano Competition). You should also note other special abilities, such as "Fluent in French," or "Designed own Web site." These sorts of activities will reflect well on you whether or not they are job-related.

You can either include your references or simply note, "References Upon Request." Be sure to ask your references permission to use their name, and alert them to the fact that they may be contacted, before you include them on your résumé. For more information on résumé writing, check out Web sites such as http://www.resume.monster.com.

Craft Your Cover Letter

When you apply for a job either online or by mail, it's appropriate to include a cover letter. A cover letter lets you convey extra information about yourself than doesn't fit or isn't always appropriate in your résumé. For instance, in a cover letter, you can and should mention the name of anyone who referred you to the job. You can go into some detail about the reason you're a great match, given the job description. You can also address any questions that might be raised in the potential employer's mind (for instance, a gap in your résumé). Don't, however, ramble on. Your cover letter should stay focused on your goal: to offer a strong, positive impression of yourself and persuade the hiring manager that you're worth an interview. Your cover letter gives you a chance to stand out from the other applicants and sell yourself. In fact, 23 percent of hiring managers say a candidate's ability to relate his or her experience to the job at hand is a top hiring consideration, according to a CareerBuilder.com survey.

You can write a positive, yet concise cover letter in three paragraphs: An introduction containing the specifics of the job you're applying for; a summary of why you're a good fit for the position and what you can do for the company; and a closing with a request for an interview, your contact information, and thanks. Remember to vary the structure and tone of your cover letter. For instance, don't begin every sentence with "I."

Ace Your Interview

Preparation is the key to acing any job interview. This starts with researching the company or organization you're interviewing with. Start with the firm, group, or agency's own Web site. Explore it thoroughly, read about their products and services, their history, and sales and marketing information. Check out their news releases, links that they provide, and read up on, or Google, members of the management team to get an idea of what they may be looking for in their employees.

Sites such as http://www.hoovers.com enable you to research companies across many industries. Trade publications in any industry (such as *Food Industry News*, *Hotel Business*, and *Hospitality Technology*) are also available at online or in hard copy at many college or public libraries. Don't forget to make a phone call to contacts you have in the organization to get a better idea of the company culture.

Preparation goes beyond research, however. It includes practicing answers to common interview questions:

* *Tell me about yourself.* Don't talk about your favorite bands or your personal history; give a brief summary of your background and interest in the particular job area.
* *Why do you want to work here?* Here's where your research into the company comes into play; talk about the firm's strengths and products or services.

✴ *Why should we hire you?* Now is your chance to sell yourself as a dependable, trustworthy, effective employee.

✴ *Why did you leave your last job?* Keep your answer short; never bad-mouth a previous employer. You can always say something simple, such as, "It wasn't a good fit, and I was ready for other opportunities."

Rehearse your answers, but don't try to memorize them. Responses that are natural and spontaneous come across better. Trying to memorize exactly what you want to say is likely to both trip you up and make you sound robotic.

As for the actual interview, to break the ice, offer a few pleasant remarks about the day, a photo in the interviewer's office, or something else similar. Then, once the interview gets going, listen closely and answer the questions you're asked, versus making any other point that you want to convey. If you're unsure whether your answer was adequate, simply ask, "Did that answer the question?" Show respect, good energy, and enthusiasm, and be upbeat. Employers are looking for workers who are enjoyable to be around, as well as good workers. Show that you have a positive attitude and can get along well with others by not bragging during the interview, overstating your experience, or giving the appearance of being too self-absorbed. Avoid one-word answers, but at the same time don't blather. If you're faced with a silence after giving your response, pause for a few seconds, and then ask, "Is there anything else you'd like me to add?" Never look at your watch and turn your cell phone off before an interview.

Near the interview's end, the interviewer is likely to ask you if you have any questions. Make sure that you have a few prepared, for instance:

✴ *"Tell me about the production process."*

✴ *"What's your biggest short-term challenge?"*

✴ *"How have recent business trends affected the company?"*

✴ *"Is there anything else that I can provide you with to help you make your decision?"*

✴ *"When will you make your hiring decision?"*

During a first interview, never ask questions like, "What's the pay?" "What are the benefits?" or "How much vacation time will I get?"

Find the Right Look

Appropriate dress and grooming is also essential to interviewing success. For business jobs and many other occupations, it's appropriate to come to an interview in a nice (not stuffy) suit. However, different fields have various dress codes. In the music business, for instance, "business casual" reigns for many jobs. This is a slightly modified look, where slacks and a jacket are just fine for a man, and a nice skirt and blouse and jacket or sweater are acceptable for a woman. Dressing overly "cool" will usually backfire.

In general, tend to all the basics from shoes (no sneakers, sandals, or overly high heels) to outfits (no short skirts for women). Women should also avoid attention-getting necklines. Keep jewelry to a minimum. Tattoos and body jewelry are becoming more acceptable, but if you can take out piercings (other than a simple stud in your ear), you're better off. Similarly, unusual hairstyles or colors may bias an employer against you, rightly or wrongly. Make sure your hair is neat and acceptable (consider getting a haircut). Also go light on the makeup, self-tanning products, body scents, and other grooming agents. Don't wear a baseball cap or any other type of hat, and by all means, take off your sunglasses!

Beyond your physical appearance, you already know to be well bathed to minimize odor (leave your home early if you tend to sweat, so you can cool off in private), use a breath mint (especially if you smoke) make good eye contact, smile, speak clearly using proper English (or Spanish), use good posture (don't slouch), offer a firm handshake, and arrive within five minutes of your interview. (If you're unsure of where you're going, Mapquest or Google Map it and consider making a dry run to the site so you won't be late.) First impressions can make or break your interview.

Remember to Follow Up

After your interview, send a thank-you note. This thoughtful gesture will separate you from most of the other candidates. It demonstrates your ability to follow through, and it catches your prospective employer's attention one more time. In a 2005 Careerbuilder.com survey, nearly 15 percent of 650 hiring managers said they wouldn't hire someone who failed to send a thank-you letter after the interview. Thirty-two percent say they would still consider the candidate, but would think less of him or her.

So do you hand write or e-mail the thank you letter? The fact is that format preferences vary. One in four hiring managers prefer to receive a thank-you note in e-mail form only; 19 percent want the e-mail, followed up with a hard copy; 21 percent want a typed hard-copy only, and 23 percent prefer just a handwritten note. (Try to check with an assistant on the format your potential employer prefers). Otherwise, sending an e-mail and a handwritten copy is a safe way to proceed.

Winning an Offer

There are no sweeter words to a job hunter than, "We'd like to hire you." So naturally, when you hear them, you may be tempted to jump at the offer. *Don't.* Once an employer wants you, he or she will usually give you some time to make your decision and get any questions you may have answered. Now is the time to get specific about salary, benefits, and negotiate some of these points. If you haven't already done so, check out salary ranges for your position and area of the country on sites such as Payscale.com, Salary.com, and Salaryexpert.com (basic info is free; specific requests are not). Also find out what sort of benefits similar jobs offer. Then don't be afraid to negotiate in a diplomatic way. Asking for better terms is reasonable and expected. You may worry that asking the employer to bump up his or her offer may jeopardize your job, but handled intelligently, negotiating for yourself may in fact be a way to impress your future employer and get a better deal for yourself.

After you've done all the hard work that successful job-hunting requires, you may be tempted to put your initiative into autodrive. However, the efforts you made to land your job—from clear communication to enthusiasm—are necessary now to pave your way to continued success. As Danielle Little, a human-resources assistant, says, "You must be enthusiastic and take the initiative. There is an urgency to prove yourself and show that you are capable of performing any and all related tasks. If your manager notices that you have potential, you will be given additional responsibilities, which will help advance your career." So do your best work on the job, and build your credibility. Your payoff will be career advancement and increased earnings.

Index